StepTrouble

William L. Coleman

CompCare® Publishers

3850 Annapolis Lane, Suite 100
Minneapolis, Minnesota 55447

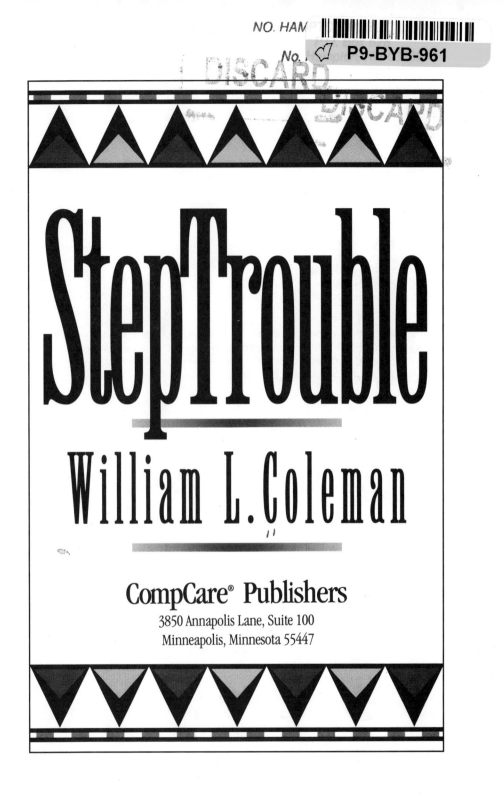

©1993 William L. Coleman
All rights reserved.
Published in the United States
by CompCare Publishers,
a division of Comprehensive Care Corporation.

Library of Congress Cataloging-in-Publication Data

Coleman, William L.,
  Step trouble: a survival guide for teenagers with stepparents/William L. Coleman.
  p. cm.
  Summary: Offers advice for teenagers on how to cope with their own feelings and new circumstances when they become part of a stepfamily.
  ISBN 0-89638-285-0
  1. Stepchildren—Juvenile literature. 2. Stepparents—Juvenile literature. [1. Stepfamilies. 2. Stepchildren. 3. Stepparents. 4. Parent and child.] I. Title.
  HQ777.7.C64 1993
  306.874—dc20   92-39637
                                                          CIP
                                                           AC

Cover design by Chris Garborg

Inquiries, orders, and catalog requests should be addressed to:
CompCare Publishers
3850 Annapolis Lane, Suite 100
Minneapolis, MN 55447
Call toll free 800/328-3330
or 612/559-4800

6   5   4   3   2   1
98   97   96   95   94   93

Contents

Thanks...

to the many teenagers, families, and groups who shared their experiences. Their stories were heart-warming, heartbreaking, and encouraging. Grandparents made me laugh and cry. Parents spoke about their hopes and frustrations. Teenagers expressed hostilities, a sense of betrayal, and their dreams for happiness.
I especially want to thank Cary, Toni, and Tuti, who brightened my outlook and reminded me how important this book could be. All the stories are faithful to the facts, but they have been changed enough to protect the participants.

Getting It Together

With a hundred other things going on, it's hard to blend into a new family. New parents, stepsiblings, a new home—it's almost like having bombs blowing up all around you.

I remember what it was like to watch my father remarry. I remember the confusion; but I also saw how much his marriage enriched our lives.

If stepteens will learn what to expect and be willing to fit in, they can save themselves a lot of grief. They can also play a major role in uniting their stepfamily and watching them become a group of people who help each other.

Stepfamilies, like any other family, take work. Oftentimes those who make the effort smile and say how much they appreciate their new families.

Give it a shot. You might be surprised at how good it can be.

Bill Coleman

Feeling Cheated

When a teenager is finally starting to become his own person, he doesn't need a lot of family turmoil. It's time to think about cars, careers, school, clothes, friends, graduation, and the future. He doesn't want family members leaving and new family members popping up. Young people have enough adjustments without family uncertainty.

It's like sixteen-year-old Rick said: "I have enough trouble getting my own stuff together, and now my mom says everything might change. She might marry this guy and then move to his house. What am I supposed to do? Give up my school, my friends, the whole bit? They act like I'm nothing."

That probably isn't the way Rick's mother felt. She thought she was doing him a big favor. Finally Rick could get the father he needed; she could get the husband she wanted; and they could move up to a better neighborhood. The problem was that she didn't see Rick's needs the same way Rick saw them. And since they didn't spend enough time talking about the situation, Rick felt left out.

Dumped on

It's easy to feel dumped on when no one talks to you. None of us likes to have someone else carve out our future without giving us a vote. When someone says, "I know what you need and this is what I'm going to do about it," we feel cheated.

Sometimes parents do know what their teenager needs. Most parents are smart people who love their families. But no one totally understands another individual's needs unless they talk about them together.

When a young person is ignored or informed after the decision is made, she feels abused. Even if the parent tries hard to explain the situation, that isn't enough. The teenager wants to be part of the decision-making process. After all, it's her life.

Teenagers know all of that. Stepparenting puts them on a roller coaster and the ride can become tiresome.

Out of control

All of us want some control over our own lives. But we can't always have it. Teachers tell us what to do; so do coaches, police, parents, and movie ushers. But we don't like being totally twisted around. When we feel completely controlled, we want to rebel. When we think our families have us in straitjackets, we want to tear loose. Teenagers are too old to be treated like little children.

Every person needs to know he has some say in how his life will be run. If we're moving to Cleveland, we want to be asked how we feel about the change.

Teenagers need to tell their parents that they want to be

part of the decision-making circle. Your parents may assume you don't want to know or you shouldn't know. They have spent years treating you like a small child and they may need to be reminded that you are maturing rapidly.

Don't throw a tantrum or lash out in frustration. Calmly and pointedly tell your parents you care very much. Where you live and whom you live with are extremely important. While you don't want to control the decision-making process, neither do you want to be dealt out.

Parents sometimes say silly things like

> *"Oh, don't worry about Sara; she gets along with everybody."*

> *"Moving is no problem. I don't think Kevin likes it here, anyway."*

> *"Cindy could help her new stepfather with his book work."*

They want to imagine the family as happy and harmonious. Consequently they assume everything will be fine without taking the time to check with everyone.

Like his teenager, the parent also feels out of control. In an attempt to handle all the loose ends, he sometimes assumes too much. In his eagerness to make everything work, he may have forgotten to touch all the bases.

When you feel cheated

If you feel like your pocket has been picked and life's happiness is being stolen away from you, there are some things you can do about it. You can't do everything to correct a bad situation, because we all get cheated. But try a few simple steps so you aren't overwhelmed.

1. Admit that it stinks

Say it out loud to your friends, to your parents, to yourself, to God. The deal is rotten and you're fed up. Express yourself. Be fairly civil, though. Don't set the couch on fire.

When we stifle our feelings or pretend everything is good when it's terrible, we only let it build up. Then later we feel like blowing.

2. Be specific

Not everything stinks, so don't exaggerate. If you don't like your stepsister but your stepmother is cool, say so. You may not enjoy the new house, but the new boat is swift. Words like "everything," "always," and "never" are usually stretching the facts.

The best way to correct a problem is to identify it. Try to avoid sweeping statements that condemn everything.

3. Be fair

Don't be afraid to compliment. Thank everyone for the good things, the thoughtfulness, and the effort. Parents and stepparents are thrown off if they think you are being unfair. Aim for sweet reasonableness.

Make your family feel good about themselves if you can, because the criticism you are about to offer could make them feel bad. Few people are totally bad, so don't make them feel that way.

4. Be a good listener

After you explain what you think stinks, sit still and listen. To simply complain and then refuse to listen is harmful. Don't try to hurt people. Try to solve problems.

Everyone needs to be a good listener. That's
true of both adults and teenagers.

5. A plan of action

The problem is out in the open. Your feelings are on the
table, and everyone has had a say. They know you feel
cheated and left out.

Next, decide what to do about it. Allow time for everyone
to make suggestions. You probably will want to meet a
second time to discuss it. That's problem-solving. You
now have the hope of making things better.

Frankly, some people don't want to solve their problems.
They enjoy pouting about feeling cheated. That probably
isn't true of you or you wouldn't be reading this book.
There definitely is hope for anyone who is willing to try to
change his or her situation.

Breaking Away

Young people like to see their circles get wider. They want more independence, more individuality, more freedom to roam. Teenagers are searching to discover who they are. They want a family connection, but not a tight one. Space is important. Breathing room is high on their list.

While the teenager is pushing for a wider circle, his parent gets married and a stepparent arrives. Suddenly the adults announce that everyone is going to become a happy, close-knit family. Biological parent, stepparent, stepbrother, a German shepherd, and Louis, the cat, are all going to watch TV, make caramel corn, and go bowling together.

The parents have a picture of a fire roaring in the hearth and everyone cozying up together on the rug The teenagers see themselves heading out the door, cruising, hanging out, and coming home late.

One reason the stepfamily might be hard to coordinate is that they are using different mental pictures. Unity and closeness are important to the parents. Transition and expansion are the teenager's goals.

Can these two diverse and opposite dreams live together under the same roof? Can parent and teen still manage to meet each other's needs? Can they prosper and appreciate each other?

The answer to those questions is yes, but it isn't easy. Millions face each other, determined to have their own way, and they crash like two trains on a single mountain track. But those who are willing to try usually build a workable relationship and often a loving one, too.

Getting your own way

Teenagers don't have to apologize for wanting to break away. It's natural. Young people don't want to be exactly like their parents. Parents wear funny clothes, listen to slow music, and take naps. Teenagers want to find out for themselves who they are.

But if they break away and don't care whom they hurt in the process, they do serious damage to the people they love. Breaking away has to be done in an orderly way and within limits; otherwise, it is simple

Teenagers are usually very caring people. Most look out for their friends, enjoy children, and like animals. If some teens wear a brash mask, it probably isn't because they are hard-hearted.

If they want to do the least amount of damage as they break away, they have to consider the needs of others in the family. Teenagers may feel overwhelmed with their own problems, but they can still show love for their families—even their broken and mended families.

Often young people have gone to their parents and asked how they could help. Sensitive and loving teenagers have proven to be good listeners and great at reassuring parents who are under tremendous stress. Most young people are not totally self-centered.

Important guidelines

How can you break away without breaking up the family? Try these guidelines. They should lessen the pressure.

1. Once a week, do something you don't want to do

If you don't like hanging around the table and talking after meals, force yourself to do it once a week. Do it just because you know it's nice.

Maybe that doesn't fit you, so do something else. Human beings can do things they don't want to do. Kindness is giving in without being told.

2. Attend big family events

You may not want to do everything with your family because you're not a kid anymore. But don't completely separate yourself from the people you love. That makes it doubly hard to reenter the circle when you want back in.

When there is a family picnic at Uncle Vern's, a wedding for cousin Stacey, or a funeral for your great-aunt, be sure to show up. When you don't show up for the big events, you cause a big strain on everyone involved. Your parents get tense, your relatives are bewildered, and your stepparent wonders what your absence means.

Relationships go smoother if you make it to the biggies. You may not want to hang out at the fast-food place with your family, but make connections.

3. Tell your family not to take it personally

Most parents are just as confused by your behavior as you are. The fact is, young people break away because they are trying to reject childhood. They probably love their parents tremendously but are afraid to let on.

Take a risk and tell your parents you love them. They don't know what's happening.

Practice short sentences like

> *"Mom, I love you, but right now I've got to have my space."*

> *"Hey, I'll stay in tomorrow night, but tonight I'm going to go out. Deal?"*

> *"I don't know why I said that yesterday. Sometimes I get carried away."*

When you can't think of what to say, put your arms around your parent and simply hold on. A decent hug can say a lot when we feel lost for words.

4. Remember, parents are not the enemy

What stops you from becoming your own person? If you think it is your parents, mark that answer wrong. If you ship your parents off tomorrow, you still won't have the freedom you are looking for. Time may stop you, maturity may stop you, education may stop you, but parents are not the obstacles.

Maturity is a process that needs a number of ingredients.

If a teenager goes to war against her parents and stepparents, she usually fights the wrong enemy. Most of the time a teenager's explosive behavior is the biggest hindrance to her own sense of maturity.

Don't look at a stepparent as another threat to your freedom. Mellow out; accept a stepparent for who he is. Lower your weapon and take him out of your sights.

5. Keep in touch

While you are trying to go into your own orbit, don't lose contact with the people who love you. Finding your way is risky business.

Keep contact. The goal is not to totally separate yourself. Talk! Be available! Care! It's lonely out there by yourself. Stay on the same wavelength with the people you love.

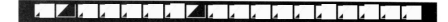

Rapid Changes

Melanie's problem: four pairs of tennis shoes and none of them fit. It wasn't just that styles were changing, but her feet were changing, too. She felt her feet were like tree roots spreading across a sprawling lawn.

That wasn't the only part of her that was expanding. After Melanie hit twelve, her body began taking strange twists and turns. Not only were its proportions changing, but so was her appetite. One day she ate like a bird and the next she chomped through the refrigerator like an Oriental wrestler.

The teen years don't need added agitation. Young people have enough bewilderment to keep them confused. Often self-conscious, they try to hide parts of their bodies. Watch a teenager sitting in a chair pull his feet back in an attempt to hide them. Have you ever seen someone folding her hands into each other for fear someone will notice how large they are?

As a teenager I remember standing in front of a mirror, wondering how my ears had grown so large. Embarrassed by a shadowy beard, I was afraid to go outside. I knew everyone was laughing at me. My voice was given to fits of squeaks and barks—one minute high, the next minute low.

Young people look for stability. Too much is happening and changing. Very little appears to be dependable. The last thing they want or need is for their families to fall apart, bounce around, and regroup. A family should be a rock, and that rock should not roll over. But families do fall apart. And often that makes a teenager really angry.

Social change

Along with self-consciousness come those frightening social events. Skating, bowling, swimming, travel camp, picnics, and dating come rushing in. What do you wear? Where do you go? Where do you stand, and what in the world do you say? It is the beginning of something wonderful but, as with most changes, the early efforts are terribly awkward.

When the social events begin, no one wants upheaval at home. You want everyone to think your family is cool. Fighting parents or splitting parents are bad news. Dating parents, marrying parents, and blending parents can be a lot of work. What teenagers really want is for everyone to hunker down and act stable.

A teenager is usually stressed out trying to discover where he fits into this mysterious world. He doesn't want the added pressure of parents who are stressed out, too. When a teen has dating problems, she doesn't want her parents to have dating problems at the same time. If a young person comes home crying because she broke up, she doesn't expect to find her parent crying for the same reason.

But it happens

Teenagers want to come home and talk about their social problems. Instead they come home and listen to their parent's social problems.

It may not be fair, but it's true. Too often a young person is forced to face his conflicts alone. He feels betrayed. He had hoped for a mother and a father to help him through the land mines of social adjustment. Now he feels cheated because that neat little family package isn't available.

Emotional change

Today's teenager is often in an emotional whirlpool. Happiness, despair, anxiety, hope, anger, contentment, fear, and uncertainty are all swirling around in a dizzying mix. Are you supposed to be macho, a charmer, a feminist, sensitive, steady, fun-loving, combative, gentle, patient, assertive, aggressive, compliant, an activist, or what?

One day everything is under control. The next day you feel like your head is stuck in a greasy, hot, kernel-exploding popcorn popper.

Emotions can be difficult to control. When they are complicated by unrest at home, emotions can become unpredictable.

Occasionally remind yourself that this is normal. When you feel like screaming, don't imagine that you are losing your mind. The need for outbursts will subside and life will go on. Your family is not crazy and neither are you.

Spiritual change

Despite the poor image projected on television and in the movies, teenagers often feel a great need for spiritual connection. Far from being raging rebels, millions of teens find churches or spiritual homes that make them feel accepted and comfortable.

Young people are spiritually hungry. One of the main reasons for this extra drive may be the problem of rapid change. Since so many areas of their lives are moving so quickly, teenagers long for some sense of stability. They are looking for a rock that does not move—something they can count on. Their deep need for security is met by their spiritual or religious beliefs.

Teenagers also welcome the message of acceptance. Since they feel awkward and unlovable, they usually respond well to those who accept them unconditionally. Some days they feel rejected by their friends, family, and authority figures. Ultimately they reject themselves. They are happy to hear about those who love them on the good days and on the bad. Unconditional love from others gives them a feeling of hope in themselves and the future.

Family change

If a family is going to break up and rebuild into a second family, the timing couldn't be worse for the average teenager. As Mark explained it: "I was fifteen and had my learner's permit. I was also trying to get up enough nerve to ask this girl out. Then, boom, my mom announces that she is going to remarry. That sounded great for her but my world was shot to pieces. Off we ran to another house, another community, another school, just like I was nobody. And she expected me to be grateful because she went out and got me a new dad."

Not every teenager feels terrible about the break-up. Some are weary from the long bickering and are relieved when it finally ends. I know I was. Others are seriously shaken and have trouble adjusting to the loss.

Change is difficult under most circumstances. The creation of a stepfamily can be one of life's most challenging changes. The good news is that the transition can be made and can produce positive, even wholesome results. Not every young person enjoys making the adjustment, but many do. The question is how this change can be made as healthy as possible.

What About the Future?

Rita was stunned when her fourteen-year-old son, Rick, asked: What about the future? She had no idea he felt so strongly about all that was going on. He asked her to call off her wedding.

Rick wanted to know how this new guy in their lives would affect Rick's plans for the future. Next year Rick would enter high school and get involved in track. In a couple of years he wanted to buy a car. Then there was the question of college. Couldn't his mother wait four or five years before going through with this big step?

There is something fearful about the future when new characters enter the scene. High school has enough pitfalls of its own without someone else to rock the boat.

Though it was a shock, Rita was fortunate. Rick was courageous enough to tell her how he felt. His mother needed that information. Now she had the opportunity to share information with him, too. She needed to spell out what Rick could expect the future to be like. No crystal ball reader, she could at least talk about goals, expectations, and hopes. Rita might also have to burst some of Rick's balloons, but at least they could become realistic about the possibilities.

Every teenager deserves a look into the future. If the parent doesn't speak up first, the young person may have to start a conversation. Don't live in silence. Don't try to guess what is going to happen. Don't stifle your fears and hope everything will work out. Every family needs open discussion about the close future. Honest concerns have to be voiced so plans can be made. Speak up! Tell the family what you are thinking and what you need to know. If they can't answer you immediately, you have given them something to think about.

Lifestyle

If a family can split, seemingly overnight, and later a new family appears, then almost anything can happen. What next? Will someone join the Foreign Legion or will your Uncle Fred become the president of Norway? What new surprise awaits you just over the next hill?

With the development of a stepfamily, certain lifestyle changes are bound to occur. Finances may be considerably different. Incomes may go up or down. Even more importantly, attitudes toward money could alter dramatically. There could be an increase in income but a decrease in cash flow.

Previously you may have had an allowance, cash for clothes, extra money for special events, and now those wells could dry up. Yesterday your mother may have controlled the purse strings, but today your stepfather might be the family accountant. Tomorrow you could be working part time and furnishing most of your own spending money.

Most of us are flexible and can adapt to new circumstances. The important thing is to know the ground rules. Tell your parents you want to discuss finances. It's too painful to wait and see what will pop up next.

Don't be surprised if all of this takes time. The guidelines are likely to shift as you get to know each other. Most situations work better when everyone throws in their opinions early.

Young people have a right to know some of the financial arrangements but not necessarily all. Is someone paying out child support? Is someone receiving child support? Are the payments being paid regularly? How are support payments being spent? Are all monies being used currently, or is something being set aside for you and the other children? Is some lump sum designated for you later?

Finances seem like a greater problem in stepfamilies than in traditional ones. Usually more people are involved under more stressful conditions. That doesn't mean the money can't be worked out in a satisfactory way. But usually it takes effort, cooperation, and lots of talk, talk, talk.

Cars, buses, and trains

At this age you're probably thinking about wheels. You already know when you can get a learner's permit and you are excited about the freedom of driving. You can picture a car in the not-too-distant future.

In your dream, how does the car arrive? If you picture it floating out of the sky on a parachute, wake up and look at reality. Will money to buy the car come out of your own pocket? Is there a family car that you think is waiting for you? Maybe you will still be riding the bus because you misunderstood the plan.

When you get close to learner's permit time, be sure to hold a vehicle conference with your family. Don't assume too much. The game plan has changed, and so have some of the team members. Expect new wrinkles to develop. Don't depend on what your parents said when you were twelve. Get the facts.

Education

With the remarriage, your future education plans may either have improved considerably or hit the rocks. Find out what everyone is thinking. You don't want to hear bad news the day you graduate from high school.

Sometimes young people think their parents "owe" them college. But a parent or stepparent may not see it that way at all.

Attitudes might change over the next few years, but you want to tie into the decision-making process. You may not get an equal vote in this campaign, but make sure you contribute some serious input.

Home base

As your move-out day approaches, who will maintain a place you can call home? Look around for the best situation. Which parent has enough acceptable space? During the first few years after high school, young people frequently move back home for weekends, summers, even years. Keep this in mind. As families fluctuate, so does space. Are your parents considering moving into larger quarters, smaller ones, or staying in the same place? How will that affect you?

Parents like to brush off future decisions by making sweeping statements like, "Oh, don't worry; everything will work out." It probably will. But young people should have some inkling as to how it will work out.

Teenagers have limited control over their immediate future. They appreciate as much information and as great a feeling of security as they can rake up.

Whom Do You Blame?

Ted was seldom home, and when he was he seemed to argue constantly with his wife, Deanna. One evening, after a particularly heated exchange, Ted packed his suitcase, left the house, and slammed the door behind him.

Their daughter, Katie, will always remember that traumatic scene. She wonders why her father did such a terrible thing. Why was he gone so often when he did live at home? Why did he leave and never move back in? Who actually filed for divorce? She doesn't see him often now and she wonders why. He always seemed like a good father to Katie when he was around.

A year later, Katie's mother married Bernie. He tries to be a decent stepfather, but Katie feels like she doesn't quite click with him. Why did all of this happen? Whose fault is it that Katie's life is such a mess?

When we feel sorry for ourselves, as most of us sometimes do, we try to figure out whom to blame.

In this mysterious investigation the clues apparently point to one or more of the following: the trouble was caused by a parent, a stepparent, God, or ourselves. Who should we blame for this tragedy?

Did a parent cause it?

Maybe. It's possible that one parent had such outrageous behavior that the other parent could no longer live with him or her. There might have been mental, physical, or sexual abuse going on. One parent may have been using too much alcohol. Possibly someone found a new love interest and was no longer faithful.

Some marriages fall apart simply because the couple is bored. They no longer see any reason to stay together.

Whatever the contributing factors, who is to say for certain? What if both parents were hurting the relationship? Who can know all the facts?

Even if we knew all about it, what would this change? After we have assembled all the clues, what will be different? We need to get on with our lives and make the most of today.

If you want to know what caused the divorce, feel free to ask. Your parents may want you to know as many facts as possible. Some things you should know so you can fit together all the pieces of the puzzle, but others may always be a mystery. Of course, some parents may prefer not to talk to you about it.

Let your parents know you are ready to listen. Then let them open up as much as they feel free to share. They may not be exactly sure how it happened.

Don't expect an answer like 2 + 2 = 4. Answers to life's complicated problems don't usually come in neat little packages. But if you want to know, be sure to ask. Also be sure to ask each parent for an explanation.

Did a stepparent cause it?

A few young people are suspicious that the stepparent is the problem. If so, they usually believe that the remarriage prevents their biological parents from reuniting. Teenagers may hate to see a parent remarry because it finalizes the split and slams the door on the family as they once knew it.

"They could have worked it out," Melanie was exasperated. "I know it could have happened, but along comes this Bob guy. Presto, it's over. If he had only stayed out of the picture."

As illogical as this sounds, many teens believe it. That's one reason why they are hostile toward their stepparents. Stepparents represent a huge boulder blocking the possibility of reconciliation.

Often these are not the facts. Very few divorced couples remarry their former partners. It happens so seldom that it almost falls into the fairy tale category. Often teenagers are slow to accept that reality.

Sometimes young people try to sabotage their stepfamilies in hopes that they can rebuild their biological or traditional families. Their goals are understandable. Their hearts have been broken. Unfortunately, attempts to rewrite history only end in disaster.

Reality is now. In the best of worlds we make the present situation as fulfilling as possible.

Did God cause it?

For many, but not all, the question arises as to whether God caused the divorce and eventually the remarriage. The other side of the coin asks why God didn't stop the divorce and remarriage ("Why didn't God do something?").

Naturally, if we don't believe in a personal God this won't be a problem. But for the people who do, this can be a serious and nagging dilemma.

Many of us feel this way but are afraid to admit it. Actually it's all right to be ticked at God. By admitting it, we are able to verbalize our feelings and resolve them. If we pretend that we never get upset, we can't get the problem off our chests.

We aren't just talking about religious people. Those who rarely darken the door of a church or synagogue might blame their problems on God in times like these. Even some who otherwise reject a personal God still look for someone to blame when things go bad.

No amount of arguing can defend God or God's actions. However, a few reminders might help:

1. God isn't interested in hurting us.
2. God doesn't cause every event.
3. God doesn't necessarily stop us every time we are in danger of hurting ourselves.
4. God is interested in bringing good things into our lives if we are willing to accept them.
5. God loves us even when we are angry at Him. When we blame Him, we build walls that separate us. If we accept God as a friend who helps, we are open to what He offers us.

Did you cause it?

This question is common among children. Children tend to believe that they make people happy and unhappy. Sometimes they think their actions control the behavior of others.

Teenagers have enough experience to know better. They are more likely to deal with the real world. They find it easier to accept divorce and remarriage as adult decisions. They think of themselves as independent individuals.

Despite their strong sense of identity, young people can still fall into the self-blame trap. They sometimes hear remarks that make them wonder. A parent may say something like

> We can't afford to keep buying clothes for this kid."

> "His late hours are driving me crazy."

> "I'm not going to be tied down to a teenager."

> "By his age I had a job."

Many teenagers have heard comments like that. Their parents may have said them without thinking, or they may have meant them. No matter what their intentions, these words do not cause divorce. All of us have problems. The question is, How do we handle those problems? Some parents deal with them by divorce or remarriage.

If a teen dropped an expensive dish and eventually the couple divorced, would you blame the dish? If athletic shoes are expensive, would you blame the expensive shoes for the divorce?

But what if you did something really serious? What if a teenager drank a great deal and got arrested and wrecked the car? Could that cause parents to divorce?

The answer is still no. A teen can create pressure on a couple, even unreasonable stress, but divorce remains an adult decision. How parents react to whatever pressures they face can cause divorce.

The blame game

Some people do cause terrible things to happen. An ax murderer may cause a death. A drunken driver can cause an accident. In some instances we can point the finger and say, "He did it." The same is true in divorce. One person can be the model spouse and the other act like a total jerk. That's possible.

But in most divorces we don't know enough of the facts to attach blame. Not all of the evidence is in, and it may never be all in.

We make lousy divorce detectives. Teenagers will be better off if they stop sniffing for clues and deal with their family situation as it is now.

Angry and Hostile

We have a right to be angry. Rotten things happen to us. We get dumped on, insulted, lied to, cheated, abandoned, ignored, crumpled up, and tossed around. Though life has a great deal to offer, sometimes it stinks. On the days when it stinks, we need to know how to handle our anger. If our anger gets out of control, we say and do things we might regret later.

The first rule of anger is to be angry. There are situations worthy of anger. That doesn't mean we go into a rage because our breakfast cereal got soggy and sank to the bottom of the bowl. You don't have to throw a fit when a sock gets lost in the laundry. But when a parent says he will pick you up Tuesday at 3:00 and he doesn't show up or call, you have reason to feel rage.

Some people think anger means we get upset and then we either stew or blow up. Many people see it as an uncontrollable emotion. Actually anger is manageable. When anger isn't managed, it often results in harm, damage, and wrecked relationships. Some people never forget the mean things that were said during an angry outburst.

The basic principle is that anger is not bad, but uncontrolled anger can be trouble.

Check the guidelines

It may seem silly to have guidelines for anger, but they are important for most of us. We feel anger and we don't know what to do about it. Consequently, many of us do the wrong thing. We either stuff our anger deep inside and let it eat away at us. Or we blow up like a geyser gone berserk.

Let's look at four guidelines that could help us deal with anger.

1. Don't get angry quickly

Some people have a habit of getting angry. It becomes a personality pattern. They are angry when their team loses, angry when their television show isn't on, angry when the sun doesn't come out. I had a friend who had three emotions: low anger, medium anger, and high anger. That made it tough to be around him. As Proverbs says, "A fool gives vent to his anger but a wise man keeps himself under control."

If we wanted to, we could be angry all the time. There is plenty to get upset about. But we can also choose to be mellow. We can back off and save our anger for the real biggies. If a parent or a sibling lies to us, that might tick us off. But even a lie doesn't have to send us into a rage.

Do not choose to live with a hair-trigger temper. If we have a short fuse, we are smart to talk to someone about it—a friend, a teacher, a minister, a counselor, someone who might understand and help us think it through.

During my junior high years I decided to vent my anger. For three years I got into fist fights with all kinds of people, large and small. Finally I decided that I had enough knots on my head and scars under my eyebrows. I slowed my anger down and took life more gently.

2. Ask why you are angry

We can feel it. Our face gets hot. Our body pumps. Usually we can tell if we are angry. Sometimes we don't realize how angry we appear. We may feel like we are merely upset while others see us as furious.

When we are angry we need to stop and ask ourselves why. Anger is like a fever. The fever isn't the problem. What causes the fever is the real illness. If all we do is stuff or express our anger, we haven't worked on the real disease.

Exactly what is it that causes us to be angry? Only after we answer this question can we deal with the germ that creates the problem.

Free-floating anger says we are mad and we aren't sure why. We are angry at everything. When that happens, we usually take it out on everyone and nothing seems to get better.

I received a letter from a woman who chewed me out about nothing. Finally it dawned on me that she must be angry at someone else and decided to take it out on me. She was confused about her anger.

Calm down and narrow your feelings. Complete this sentence: "Specifically I am angry about. . ." Someone didn't tell you what was going to happen? You hate switching schools? You are being abused? They took your bedroom away? No one understands you? They picked a vacation spot without asking you? Your father never calls or visits? What do you see as the problem?

Sometimes, like the woman who wrote me, you may act angry about the use of the bathroom when you are actually resentful that your mother has someone else in her life. Anger can be tricky business.

3. Express your anger

This isn't easy and may take some practice. We need to go to the person who upset us and tell her we are angry at what she did. We can say it calmly, but it needs to be said. Something like:

"Could you please put the toothpaste back when you finish."

"We never talk about important things."

"You seldom call."

"No one cares how I feel."

"I wish you had asked my opinion."

Say whatever it takes! Under most conditions the best person to go to is the one who is causing the pain. You may learn that it was a misunderstanding; the person could deny what you say, or he could correct the situation. At least the matter will be aired and the two of you could have more respect for each other. Don't shut down and don't blow up. Vent it!

In some cases the person you need to talk to might be dangerous. If necessary, talk to someone else about how to approach the situation.

When you express your anger, be direct, be firm, and let the person respond. Don't merely shout at him and stomp off.

4. Keep your anger short

It is all right to get angry, but it is not all right to stay angry. Over a long period of time anger eats away and hurts the hostile person, those we are mad at, and other innocent people.

Too often people punch someone in the nose over something they have been angry about for ten years. We need to express our anger in an acceptable way and then drop it. This rule of thumb still holds here: "Do not let the sun go down while you are still angry."

Remind yourself to identify your anger, speak up, and then drop the matter. If the problem continues, do something about it again. But don't let your anger keep boiling.

Anger is normal. The best of us want to blow our stacks sometime. By handling anger correctly, we can turn it into a positive force and get things changed.

You're No Child

You know teenagers and children are drastically different. Unfortunately, some parents forget the differences and try to lump everyone together. All of us deserve respect. Respect for our personalities, respect for our dreams, and respect for our stage in life. If each person is not treated as an individual with separate needs, problems are created.

Children and older teenagers often adapt to a stepfamily better than the thirteen-to-sixteen-year-old group. While children are individuals, they are less independent and seem to accept the home surroundings more easily. Parents may also be more likely to communicate better with this age. The average seventeen-, eighteen-, or nineteen-year-old probably takes stepparenting better because he sees himself on the way out. In a couple of years, she will either be working or at college and won't really see herself as "homebound."

Thirteen-to-sixteen-year-olds are in double turmoil. Their lives are already in a stage of upheaval. Entry into adolescence has always been difficult. Hormones are raging, acne is breaking out, and their social scene is in constant turmoil. When these eruptions are mixed into the blender of a new stepfamily, the normal difficulties of living become almost unmanageable.

This is no time to be treated like a child. It is no time to try to step back and "start all over again." Teenagers are too far down the track to act as if their first family never existed. They are becoming too mature, too complicated, too sophisticated to go back.

That's why it hurts when teens are treated like children. Sometimes they have to gently remind their parents and stepparents that this is the case. While teens are not adults, neither are they playing T-ball. They need to be addressed and dealt with where they are.

Blending sounds terrible

On the one hand, two families are trying to blend or meld into one. On the other hand, a teenager is busy attempting to discover his own identity. The two concepts are exclusive.

A teen hears a parent's voice chanting, "Blend in, blend in." At the same time her inner voice is saying, "Stand out, stand out, be yourself." Those conflicting messages can drive anyone crazy.

Blending has a bad sound to it for many young people. It's like making pudding. Everything is poured into a bowl and stirred up until it looks colorless and shapeless. Instead of applauding individuality, the very process destroys identity. It is as though a person becomes nobody as she becomes part of the group.

What young people want is to hold on to their individuality and yet be part of the group. They look for independence and dependency. Hard to define and just as difficult to accomplish.

While teenagers want to feel self-reliant, too often their behavior suggests that they need guidance and direction. The problem comes when they insist on being treated as mature individuals, but their actions are immature.

Marks of maturity

People of all ages have trouble with maturity sometimes. Fifty-year-olds leave the milk out, scream at small problems, and break their promises once in a while. But there are some basic marks of maturity that should be apparent. If a young person wants to be accepted as fairly mature he should demonstrate a few of these traits:

- Keep your word.
- Respect others.
- Follow through on projects.
- Act without being reminded.
- Be on time.
- Show emotional stability.
- Tell the truth.
- Accept responsibility for your actions.

We can't simply announce that we are mature. Our behavior has to support that claim. Anyone who constantly screams, leaves jobs half done, slams doors, doesn't show up for meals, and lies to cover his tracks has to be treated like a child. A very young child.

Our age does not guarantee maturity. Our actions speak very loudly about how we ought to be treated.

Need for privacy

With the mixing and matching of families there is frequently the loss of space. Someone moves out every other weekend; another person moves in. On some holidays the house is packed; on others it's empty. Two teenagers move in for the summer; a nine-year-old lives there for two weeks. And so it goes.

Stepfamilies frequently shuffle children and teens around like cards. Most houses are medium sized and can't provide for every type and combination that could happen. Four girls and one boy or three boys and two girls call for creative arrangements. If the same home has only one bathroom, it can look like the monkey house at the zoo.

No matter how many people are involved, every teenager needs privacy and space. Ideally each young person would have a room of her own. Ideal, however, can be hard to get. If she has to share a bedroom with one or two others, then certain parts of that room should be hers alone. A closet, a corner, a dresser may be sufficient. There must be an area that is hers exclusively. No one should be allowed to touch whatever is in her area.

If these spaces have not yet been defined, it's time to bring up the subject. Be kind and polite, but explain that this subject should be handled. Sit down with your parents and describe what you need. Don't be unreasonable; there may be a lot of people to consider. Once your needs are described, a family gathering can be called to work out the details. If necessary, explain this at both houses or at as many as may be involved.

You aren't aiming for a land grab, just a peace settlement. Exactly where will your diary, CDs, photos, and green shorts find a home? We'll talk more about this later.

This is good strategy: Meet, talk, explain, work it out. Bad strategy is: Sulk, pout, be silent, get bitter, hold your breath, turn blue. Other bad strategies are: Yell, scream, accuse, get even. Go for the good strategy.

When it comes to the bathroom or bathrooms, try the same approach. What "stuff" do you keep in the bathroom? Would you be better off keeping as much as possible in your dresser? Everyone who shares a bathroom can expect some inconveniences. Talk about how you can best hold those to a minimum.

Discuss time schedules. How can you adjust to make the largest number of people as happy as possible? Privacy is important. Look for slack times to take leisurely baths, wash your hair, or whatever needs extra pampering.

Be optimistic! Many siblings and stepsiblings understand each other's needs and respect each other's space. Even when they are having serious trouble with their parents, they seem to make peace with the other teens in the home. Young people live in the same culture and often communicate well.

Parents get confused

When a parent sets up a stepfamily, she has gone through a great deal of pain. Don't feel sorry for her. But try to understand her experience. Teenagers also face deep hurt during the breakup of one family and the creation of another.

Since life may be moving fast and hard, parents sometimes forget how grown up their teenagers are. Expect that. Often a parent wishes you were still a child. She wants to simply pick you up and put you in a corner. The surprise comes when she discovers that she can no longer do that. Your life and hers have become too complicated.

Other parents want you to become an instant adult. They want you to stop having problems and changes and hurry out of your teen years as fast as possible. That isn't realistic either.

If your parents sometimes lose their cool, try not to lose yours. Chill out. Be who you are at exactly the right time.

Parents will ride the roller coaster of emotions. Recognize when they are taking the big dip and try to keep your feet on the ground. Sometimes you have to go up and down, too. But the ability to recognize all of this as normal could stop you from acting goofy now and then.

Teenagers aren't children. Their role in a stepfamily is unique and needs to be accepted with mutual respect.

How to Get Along

Old convicts used to say prisoners could do either good time or bad time. If they wanted, they could fight everyone in prison and break every rule in the place. That was doing bad time. Their other choice was to try and get along. They didn't have to like everyone, but they didn't look for trouble either. That was doing good time. Each prisoner had to decide which way to go.

Stepfamilies aren't prisons, but the principle is the same. Each of us must choose whether these will be good years or bad. We can't decide for anyone else in the family, but we can select a path for ourselves.

If someone else in the family rants and raves and acts irresponsibly, that certainly is a problem. All we can do is control our own attitude.

An older brother told his sister that she was only creating trouble. Her continuous rebellion against the family kept everyone unhappy and cranky, he said. He was going to play it cool. His parents were providing well for him and were going to help with college and he saw no reason to rock the boat when he didn't need to.

Each had a choice to make: good time or bad.

In some abusive situations, conditions are truly impossible. But most are workable, especially when a young person looks for ways to get along.

We send out signals even when we don't know it. Our personality, our body language, our voice, our facial expression all have messages. They say you can come close or you had better stay away.

The porcupine fish is a great example. It swims along like any other fish until it becomes frightened. Fear causes it to puff up its sides; short quills pop up. Like tiny swords, they stick out ready to stab anything that touches it.

That works fine for fish, but it is a terrible system for people. Yet some of us act that way. When others try to get close to us, prickly quills jump out all over our personalities. When people see our quills sticking up, they stay away.

Fortunately it's possible to improve the messages we send out. In turn we can receive better messages from those around us.

Look at some of the ways we can get along.

1. Give and take

Self-centered people tend to turn off everyone else. They have to have what they want when they want it. Selfish people wreck relationships by demanding their own way most of the time.

Two-year-olds, teenagers, and adults easily get caught up in this. Some young people feel like they never get their way and no one cares about their needs. That could collapse quickly into self-pity.

First, look for ways to give. If your stepfather mows the lawn, startle him by doing it without being asked. After dinner tonight, volunteer to do the dishes. That will catch everyone off guard, and they will wonder what you have done wrong. Don't worry, pleasant shocks are good for parents. Keeps their arteries flowing.

Second, be sure to talk. Tell your family what you honestly need. You don't have to be a doormat. That isn't good for anyone. Be reasonable and clear. Parents need to know what it takes to keep you running smoothly.

2. Try to understand

Stepparents live in a different culture than their stepteens. Their lifestyle, clothes, ambitions, challenges, and tensions are not the same. Listen carefully to what interests stepparents, and try to get a view of their world.

What kind of pain have they experienced? What are their shattered dreams? What dreams do they share and aim for? Parents are also complicated people.

The call is usually for parents to try to understand teenagers. If the family is to live in peace, teenagers need to hear what parents are saying and try to comprehend the feelings behind the words.

Ask parents to explain what they mean. Be patient. Take time. Reach out for each other and learn the mysteries of stepparents.

3. Forgive

Relationships without forgiveness are not healthy. People living under the same roof are bound to rub each other the wrong way from time to time. Don't be surprised that you get upset at stepparents. They also get upset with you and with themselves.

Forgiveness is like a rope. We can use it to pull ourselves toward others. If we refuse to hold on or forgive, the rope slackens and we fall away. Keep the rope of forgiveness taut. Pull on it every time you feel yourself slipping.

We know that forgiveness is not a stepfamily problem. It is a people problem. The temptation is to think that we have trouble because we are part of a stepfamily. All families have difficulties. All family members need forgiveness sometimes.

Silently all of us could say,

> *"forgive us our sins as we have forgiven those who have sinned against us."*

Promise yourself that you won't carry the heavy burden of grudges around. A grudge will leave you tired and worn out. Drop your grudge and get to know the person.

4. Send out good vibes

Pass a smile around every chance you get. If you smile, most people will smile back. You set the tone and the atmosphere by injecting cheerfulness into your family.

"Well, if they aren't going to be happy, I'm not going to be happy either." The person who says that has dug in his heels and is waiting for someone else to cheer up.

Regardless of how other people act, each of us has the opportunity to control our own input. We need to regularly ask ourselves what we are contributing to this relationship. If we are in the bad vibes business, we spread it around and cause bad vibes in others.

None of this makes us responsible for how someone else acts. A grouchy stepmother creates her own attitude. Don't believe that she is a grump because of you. Your task is to contribute as much sunshine as possible. Your attitude can make it easier for a stepfather or stepsister, but in the final analysis everyone is accountable for her own behavior. Each of us can add to the sunshine level and reduce the gloom. That's worth a great deal.

Taking Sides

Who's right and who's wrong? Those questions keep bouncing around like Ping-Pong balls. Who started the fight? Who walked out first? Who has the worst temper and says the meanest things when the going gets tough?

It's hard to judge exactly where a relationship went bad. If you are a teenager caught in the middle, it is especially difficult to figure out what's going on.

Fortunately, young people don't have to understand who started the trouble. They don't have to discover who is innocent or find someone to blame. Divorce and remarriage are adult decisions. True, teenagers are affected by those decisions, but adults are the ones who make them. Often things are so complicated that even the parents aren't sure what caused them to happen.

Two sides

In most stories there are two different explanations. If we hear only one version, we probably don't have all the facts. Mother might tell us how terrible Father behaved, but Father may give another account. Both stories might be true, but they are seen from different points of view.

44

Maybe one parent is lying, but possibly both are telling the truth. The facts, the evidence, the testimonies would baffle even a trained judge.

Drop out of the judging business. Try to avoid taking sides. Each parent may desperately want you to agree with him or her, but don't get trapped. It's adult business. Let the adults work it out.

A stepparent and a parent sometimes tell awful tales about your other biological parent. Maybe he doesn't visit you or pay child support or call as often as he should. Possibly her lifestyle has gone to pieces. Some of that behavior might be true. But reserve judgment. Hear out both biological parents. Don't rush to condemn when you hear only part of the story.

Parents would like for you to agree with them. They want your support. That's understandable. But people can get their feelings hurt when you jump around trying to choose sides.

You aren't a stick

One parent's anger for another parent might be understandable. Maybe they have been cheated, lied to, abused, hit, belittled, or any number of other mean things. Those things happen, and they are terrible. There is nothing right about them. However, adult mistreatment of each other has to be handled by adults.

Teenagers are not sticks to be used by one parent to beat another parent. When a parent works hard to turn the child against the other parent, he is trying to hurt that parent by using the teenager. When that happens, the young person becomes confused and feels used.

Let adults fight their own battles. Adolescents have enough turmoil of their own.

Teenage heroes

As young people rush into adulthood, they want to help others, especially the ones they love. Sometimes in the worst of situations, teenagers want to act like heroes. When they see their parents arguing or their parents and stepparents arguing, they want to jump in and solve the problem.

Adults need to settle their own disputes. It's hard to bite your tongue and walk away, but that may be true heroism. You wish you had some special action or some magic words that would calm their troubled waters, but it seldom works that way. By interfering, you are likely to create bad feelings between a parent and yourself.

Be kind and thoughtful. That's usually the way to be the most helpful. Solving problems for others sounds good, but too often it only tangles us in someone else's web. It takes a great deal of courage to back off and say, "These are adult troubles, not mine."

Don't be a spy

Parents who are in pain are tempted to ask their children to do unreasonable things. One of the most unreasonable is to ask the teenager to spy on the other parent.

This may not sound like a big deal at first. They ask for something like

> *"Let me know if his girlfriend is spending the night."*

> *"Why don't you just casually ask him what he is paying for rent."*

"If she is dating that guy, I need to know."

"Is he betting big money at those poker games?"

"Let me know what she says about me."

"I want to know if he's drinking. He's not supposed to drink."

When a parent asks you to collect information and report back, she is asking you to spy. Espionage sounds intriguing, but when it is against your adult relatives, the practice is destructive. Put your magnifying glass and tape recorder away. It is unreasonable for a parent to expect her children to snoop and tell on the other parent.

Some parents disagree. They say that if a father isn't paying child support, it is in the teenager's best interest to collect information. Not true. Teenagers should not be put in the position of betraying their parents. These are adult problems and must be solved by adults.

Idealizing the other parent

The parents you live with on a regular basis are the ones who seem to have the most discipline, the most rules, and the least money. They have to work with you on a daily routine. Consequently, you might experience the most friction, the most disagreements, and the most tension with the parent you live with.

When you visit your other biological parent, living may seem easygoing and less demanding. Money might be more available, you might do more exciting things, get gifts, and go places. You may not have to help around the house, and curfew may be later. Some teenagers are treated like a guest in one home and like a worker in the other.

This is why many young people want to leave one home and move into the other. They enjoy the relaxed living and lack of responsibility. It sounds great.

When two homes are different in lifestyle, you can understand why the more generous one is appealing. Soon the teenager idealizes the family she visits the least. She dreams that someday she will permanently join the easy-going parent and live happily ever after.

The parent with the sports car, the recreational vehicle, and the loose rules looks like a touch of paradise. But what most of us really need is a parent who cares every day, sticks with us on good days and bad, and has enough sense to tell us "no" when we need to hear it.

The temptation is to choose sides and prefer the "Santa Claus" parent. Each parent can be good, but steady, dependable parents are absolutely necessary.

Try to accept each parent as he is and appreciate his real strengths. Instead of choosing sides in this parental tug-of-war, stay calm and level-headed.

Cool It!

Stepteens need to learn how to relax. They can't afford to argue over every word and every event. Family living offers plenty of opportunities to blow up and rag on each other. But losing our cool only seems to increase the confusion and to hurt everyone's feelings.

All of us need to go over the checklist from time to time. Are we running too hot too often, or are we playing it pretty cool? If the temperature is staying too high, we need to back off and sit on the ice for a while.

We are running too hot if

- We throw a magazine at the cat more than once a day.

- We blame our stepbrother for the increase in rain.

- We yell when answering simple questions.

- We have no good thoughts about our parents and stepparents.

- We feel personally attacked whenever household jobs are mentioned.

- We whine because we can't find the remote control.

- We are upset when family plans get changed.
- We steam because we can't have the special sweater.
- We complain about curfews.
- We bellyache when a parent or stepparent asks us to take out the trash.

Any signs of touchiness or oversensitivity suggest that our engine is overheating. That's often hard to see in ourselves. Sometimes we need to ask a friend if we seem wound too tightly. At other times a checklist helps.

We know we are playing it pretty cool when

- We feel grateful for people and things.
- We volunteer help before we are asked.
- We compliment our sibling or stepsibling.
- We concentrate more on what we have than on what we don't have.
- We think that God has been good.
- We find ourselves giving to others.
- We usually accept change and go with it.
- We hear people say dumb things and simply let it go.
- We admit that some people have it worse than we do.
- We accept disappointments as a natural part of life.
- We can count three blessings in our lives.
- We sometimes hum or whistle a happy tune.
- We feel good about our future.

No one feels cool all the time about everything on this list. But these serve as a measuring rod. If they are seldom true of us, we may need to question our attitude. Attitude is something we can recognize and work to improve.

Good actions can help us develop good attitudes. Don't wait until you feel cool. Start acting cool, and the feelings might just follow.

Acting cool sounds like we are pretending. We can act cool when we genuinely want to be cool. We may not feel relaxed and cooperative, but we do it anyway. The action will become the real us when we put it into force.

Do something good and you will soon start to feel good.

How to act cool

- Come in fifteen minutes before curfew.
- Straighten up the garage without being asked.
- Compliment everyone in the family—one a day.
- Turn your music volume down.
- Act excited about someone else's idea.
- Clean out the fishbowl.
- Decide to smile all day long.
- Do something for the person you don't like.
- Jump in and do the dishes.
- Say "thank you" and "please."
- Ask a parent or stepparent for advice.
- Turn to someone else's favorite television show.
- Think of more cool things for this list.

Homes and families make lousy battlefields. The people who love us are not really the enemy. Stepteens who are laid back and accepting seem to enjoy their families more.

Exactly What Is a Stepparent?

If I asked you what an alligator is and you replied that it is a lizard, you would be correct. But I still wouldn't know much. You would have to describe what the alligator looks like, how it acts, and where it lives if I am to understand what it is like. Is this lizard twelve inches long or twelve feet long? Does it eat flies, frogs, or birds?

The word stepparent is just as elusive. Is a stepparent a real parent, a pretend parent, an occasional parent, or not a parent at all? Can a stepparent tell a teenager what to do? Can a teenager tell a stepparent what to do? Do they have to give and take and try to be friends?

Originally the word *stepparent* was used for someone who took the place of a parent who died. Divorce was rare, but death—especially among childbearing women—was more frequent. That may be why fairy tales speak more often of stepmothers than of stepfathers.

Because stepmothers and stepfathers often felt less attached to the stepchildren, the term *stepchild* became a word of little respect. Recently I asked someone how a project was going, and he replied that it was being treated like a stepchild. Often stepchildren and stepteens are treated very well, but the stereotype of the neglected stepchild lingers on.

Who is a stepparent?

A stepparent is someone who agreed to marry a biological or natural parent. The biological parent is alone because she has divorced, her partner has died, or she has never married.

Most often people marry because of love, but there are other serious considerations. Parents without marriage partners may also need help with their children, finances, or personal pressures, or for a long list of other reasons. Life is complicated.

Stepparents are not adoptive parents. They don't have the same legal standing as natural or adoptive parents. Laws, however, differ from state to state.

When a parent and stepparent marry, their first priority is to each other. They might consult the teenagers before they marry, but the final decision is theirs to make. They are the ones who are pledging commitment to each other.

An authority figure

If a stepparent isn't exactly a total parent, he or she is an adult. A stepparent's presence in the home commands respect. Teenagers aren't supposed to pour pudding in their stepfather's shoes and call him "Dumb Dad."

The person carries authority for three reasons:

1. He is married to your parent.
2. He is an adult.
3. He lives under your roof and must make adult decisions.

Imagine these scenarios:

- A twenty-one-year-old brings alcohol to the house to share it with minors.
- A seventeen-year-old boy is physically beating his fourteen-year-old sister.

In either of these cases, a stepparent has the right and obligation to intervene. She received her authority because of the three reasons mentioned above. It has little to do with whether you like her or not.

The authority figure battle

Teenagers often battle over authority. Who can tell them what to do and who can't? That's one of the reasons they particularly resent getting a new parent. Usually they have enough trouble taking orders or directions from a biological parent.

Who is this person entering your life? What business does he have giving orders? With luck, the stepparent will not become the big order giver. The natural parent will become the major avenue of authority, but sometimes the stepparent has to help. The less a teenager rebels and fights that authority, the better everyone will get along.

Be fair

Sharon knew she was taking out all her frustrations on her new parent. In her mind, someone needed to pay for all the injustices she was receiving—the broken home, torn emotions, continuous upheaval. Yet Sharon couldn't bring herself to blame either her mother or her father.

She needed them. It was also too painful to accuse herself for the turmoil.

Perplexed, she dumped all of her problems on the new parent. She wasn't emotionally attached to this outsider. He wasn't part of her package. Consequently, Sharon blasted her stepfather and continued to dislike him for years. He became the easy target even if he was the wrong target.

In a marriage, the primary relationship exists between the two adults. But everyone needs to make an effort to get along. To dislike a stepparent without giving him a fair chance is prejudice in the extreme. No one should be expected to take all of the blame for our problems.

- Give them a break.
- Cut them some slack.
- Give them some relief.

Besides, when we treat people unfairly we create a lot of unfairness for ourselves. We can hardly expect someone to stand still and take all the junk we want to pile on him.

Growing into friendship

The parent and stepparent relationship began as a partnership between the two. They may have consulted you or tried to sound you out, but the final decision belonged to them. But now that they are married, the question arises as to where in the world you really fit.

In time, perhaps you and your stepparent will bond together as friends. This is a real possibility and it happens in many families.

Abraham Lincoln received a stepmother when he was about ten years old. His mother died when she was thirty-six, leaving Abe and his sister Sarah with a father who could barely care for them.

Soon their father, Tom, headed for Elizabethtown, Kentucky, to look for widow Sarah Bush Johnstone. They had known each other when they were young, and on December 2, 1819, they became husband and wife.

When stepmother Sarah moved into Lincoln's boyhood home she brought along what possessions she owned, including a few books. Abe's father considered an education a waste of time, but the new stepparent encouraged Abe to read.

Abe and his stepmother shared a kindred spirit. They knew that labor was necessary, but there was more to life than splitting logs and tilling fields. One storyteller claims that Sarah used to kid Abe that she didn't mind him tracking mud on the floor, but she hated it when he bumped his head and got the ceiling dirty. Reportedly, Abe had a barefoot boy walk in mud and then turned him upside down and had the boy walk on the ceiling. When his stepmother saw the mess she laughed and laughed. Abe, of course, washed off the footprints.

When Sarah (also called Sally) was in her seventies, her successful stepson traveled to see her in Farmington, Illinois. He was leaving soon to become President of the United States, and he wanted to bid his stepmother farewell. The two of them had established a bond that Abe and his biological father never shared. As they enjoyed each other's presence, Sarah and Abraham sensed that they might never see each other again.

Who can say what bonds of friendship and love step-relatives might find for one another? Smart people give it a chance and let it develop.

Stepparents enter the relationship with love and a need for others. Frequently their attachment spreads to the entire family, especially if the young people are open to that relationship.

Stepbrothers and Stepsisters

(The Tossed Salad Siblings)

Christmas was hard at the Pickering household. For five days Mother Pickering, Father Pickering, and their four children got together for the holidays. Angie (sixteen) and Garth (eleven) were the children of Mrs. Pickering. Nick (fifteen) was the son of Mr. Pickering. Todd (eight) was the child of Mr. and Mrs. Pickering.

Angie, Garth, and Todd lived at the Pickering home. Nick visited the home every other weekend, one month in the summer, and on some holidays. Angie and Garth visited their father under a similar arrangement.

Their situation is fairly typical of many stepfamilies. Stepsiblings are frequently moving in and out, and arrangements have to change with each shift.

The Pickerings were fortunate to have four bedrooms in their home. Each child or young person had his or her own bedroom except when Nick came to visit. Then space became complicated. Should Nick move in with Garth or Todd? Or should Garth move in with Todd, with Nick taking Garth's room?

The family couldn't afford a fifth bedroom. One alternative was to have Nick over when Angie and Garth were away, but the parents wanted them to grow up knowing each other.

Many "Tossed Salad Teenagers" are caught up in a shuffle similar to that of the Pickerings. From all the negotiations, deals, compromises, and rearrangements that must be made, some teenagers learn great personal skills. Others live in constant turmoil and dislike the shifting from place to place. Although it is hard to admit, many teenagers don't care to visit because the hassle isn't worth it.

Teen to teen

"Frankly, we don't have any trouble," Nathan told me. "Jon and I get along great. It's only when our parents get involved that everything falls apart."

Nathan and Jon get along for two major reasons. First, they live in the same culture. They understand each other. Their parents are people of another, older culture and naturally have more trouble relating to them. Second, they see themselves as survivors in the same boat. Each has been a victim of a divorce and remarriage they did not create. Consequently they can easily empathize—or feel what the other feels.

Since they can't control their situation, they have decided to chill. Each is going to relax and accept the other as he comes.

Unfortunately, not all stepsibling situations work this well. Some live under terrible friction.

If stepsiblings are close in age, there can be some terrific pluses. You might share clothes, CDs, even go places together. Teenagers can talk late into the night, rent videos, or find someplace to hang out. Most teens don't want to spend much time talking politics with their parents, no matter how cool they are.

Roadblocks to friendship

Stepteens can look for positives in a stepsibling instead of expecting trouble. Attitude and expectation will go a long way. The tension really increases if a teenager is hostile toward a parent and tries to take it out on the other teenager. The anger muddies the water and prevents them from becoming friends.

It isn't reasonable to expect all teenagers to click. In fact it's degrading to dump all the young people together and think they will get along like playful seals. Differences in personalities, tastes, hobbies, music, movies, clothes, and friends all contribute to separate mixes. Teenagers can move fairly close and become friendly even if they will never be best friends.

Areas of barriers

To produce an atmosphere where friendship can grow, a few areas have to be checked out. We mention four things to seriously consider that could help teenagers get along with their stepsiblings.

1. Space

If a stepteen dislodges a teenager from her living space, they are less likely to get along. He is set up as the ugly intruder. His existence makes life terribly uncomfortable. Space is expensive but usually not impossible to attain. Explain your anxiety about the living conditions and make a couple of sensible suggestions about how to best work things out for everyone. It could be that your parents have not thought through the space problems from your perspective.

Be flexible and look for compromise. Try not to be demanding and simply intent on getting your own way.

Things go better when the largest number of people are happy.

Ask for areas where you can safely put your things and clearly designate them as yours. Everyone needs personal zones that they can call their own.

2. Privacy

How can anyone feel secure and relaxed unless a few basic rules of privacy apply? An important part of growing up is a sense of individuality without having everything exposed to others. Whether you share a bedroom or not, several guidelines should be guaranteed.

- Other teenagers are not allowed to go through your dresser drawers without your permission.
- They may not read your diary.
- No one can take your clothing or other possessions without your permission.
- No one may enter the bathroom while you are there without your permission.

When those rules are constantly violated, siblings of all kinds end up at war. Voice your concerns and establish good ground rules. From time to time you may need to talk about them again. Under normal circumstances we are entitled to privacy.

3. Respect

A family can't always run on a vote system, but everyone's needs and concerns must be considered. Many times parents have to give commands and directives. They can't sit outside in the parking lot until everyone agrees on the restaurant. Someone has to say, "We're going in here to eat."

When a pattern of thoughtlessness regarding a person's feelings or personal needs develops, that person is not getting any respect. When you get little or no respect, you begin to think you are unimportant. No one should be made to believe she is unimportant.

Teenagers think they are not respected if:

- They are seldom included in making plans.
- They are taken for granted, with statements like, *"Oh, Roger will watch the children."*
- They are not given adequate information about the family and family changes.
- They are not trusted.
- They receive family news from nonfamily members.
- A parent's lengthy absence is not explained.
- They are treated like children.

Gently remind your parents that you are a person. Teenagers aren't a species, category, or subculture. Each one is a unique individual and should be accepted that way.

Social animals

Stepteens are made to mingle. When they visit a stepparent's home, they need plenty of social outlets. They should never be cooped up or smothered by the adults.

Since the visiting young person is in a foreign atmosphere, he needs to know what he can do and where he can go. Where can he make friends in a hurry? Church groups are often good places to mix, especially if they aren't cliquish.

If there are other teenagers at the house, they might find it easy to do things together. They shouldn't be forced, however. No young person should have to give up his weekend plans simply because his stepsibling is coming over. That kind of disruption can quickly lead to deep resentment.

A new child

Often couples who remarry want to have children of their own. They may love the children they have by their previous partners, but they also want an offspring or two from this marriage.

Don't be surprised if they have a baby, and don't be shocked if the little bundle changes your family. Sometimes the changes are for the worse and sometimes for the better. It all depends on the people involved and how they choose to react.

A baby can help draw stepsiblings together. Each teenager may thoroughly love the child and cooperate to make it happy. This child is related to each of them, and they pitch in to do what they can.

On the other hand, the baby can become a threat if they let it. A teenager might see the baby as:

- An embarrassment

  (Why did this old couple have a baby?)

- An attention stealer

  (Much time and money is directed to the baby.)

- A nuisance

  (Crying, baby-sitting, wrecking tapes, etc.)

Attitude will pretty much determine which way this one flops. If you jump in at the beginning and love the baby, the relationship could be fantastic.

The jealousy problem

In any family, jealousy can tear everyone apart. It's an ugly creature that leaps up and attacks the people around us. It makes us worry about who has the most, who gets it first, and who deserves it least.

All of us have problems. We can't find our homework, we can't fix the stereo, and our best friend keeps getting mad at us. But whatever our problems, they are made far worse when we become jealous over others. As long as we feel jealous, we will always have a tough relationship with that person.

Give it a rest. Let them have what they have. The important thing is people and not possessions. We tend to dislike anyone we are jealous of. Drop the jealousy and keep the person.

Stepsiblings can become friends forever. They share experiences that will last a lifetime.

Two Stepparents

Since most divorced people remarry, the likelihood is that teenagers will have two stepparents. Therefore, teens will need to make serious adjustments each time they move from house to house. Most teenagers learn to get along with two major adults, but often stepteens have to juggle four. It takes more skill to track four parents and check where they are.

The altitude seems to change when the teenager moves from one home to the other. It's as if home A is in the valley where the air is thick, but home B is in the mountains where the air is thin. When they visit home B they may have to go slow at first while they get used to a different atmosphere.

Stepparent A and Stepparent B may be great people. It may not be the "wicked" stepfather in the valley and the "mellow" stepmother in the mountains. They can each be terrific people and still be quite different. Smart teenagers figure out what those differences are and plan for them.

Not to compare

The big temptation is to compare stepparents like fruit. You decide that a peach is better than an apple and you reject the apple. That's putting stepparents into a win-or-lose situation like we do in sports. The fact is that both a peach and an apple can be great and we can accept both.

It's mostly mental. Refuse to pit one stepparent against the other. Don't think of one house as the winner and the other as the bummer. Each home and each stepparent has strengths of its own. Concentrate on those benefits, and in most cases both households can work for you.

This isn't easy. Sometimes people will try to make you compare. They will ask you which house you would rather visit. That isn't a fair question. Tell them so. It's important that you make each home work for the best. Don't pick sides. Get along in both households if it's possible.

Home hopping

The "grasshopper complex" is hard for adults to appreciate, especially if they have never done it. Adults move, but usually they exercise considerable control over their own living conditions. The "grasshopper" will move here for a couple of weeks, and then over there for two days, and then back here for a holiday. They seldom feel like they are in control. Under joint custody a teenager might be in home A for three weeks and then in home B for three weeks, especially if both homes are in the same school district.

Living in two homes can make a person feel like she has no home at all. Just as four parents can make a teenager feel like she has no parent.

To feel at home in two homes, three areas have to be established.

1. Good living space has to be made available, complete with things specifically for the teenager.

2. The young person must understand and try to adapt to the local rules and regulations in that home.

3. A teenager should get to know the parent and step-parent well and try to fit into their personalities while he visits. (Naturally the parents should attempt to adjust to the young person's personality at the same time.)

The good list

It's hard for me to remember things unless I write them down. There is something about the process of thinking, writing, and seeing the words that makes an impression on my memory.

Try making a good list about each home and each step-parent. Most of us are prone to say, "There's nothing good about that place." Sometimes we may honestly feel that way. But in more rational moments we can think of some great pluses. If we write them down, we remember them. That makes us feel good about the place and the people.

Second, make a list of the good qualities you find in your stepparents. Some teenagers don't want to make a list because it begins to end the war. If we end the war, we can move on to healing and happiness. Not every young person wants to end the battle. Many teenagers are fighting hard to hold on to the pain and the hurt. Happiness is a choice and often it begins by accepting the stepparents.

Once you start to identify each stepparent's "likeables," you can allow yourself to draw close and become a friend. For one stepparent that means personal conversations in the late hours; for the other stepparent it means playing Ping-Pong. This takes time, but the areas of "comfort" and "likeables" will open up if you don't move away from each other.

But aren't there some stepparents that no one can get along with? Probably so. There are some duds in every area of life. Most likely your stepparents will not be among them. Stepparents are people, and usually people have a friendly side.

There is no need for a "bad" list. It isn't helpful and only reinforces the things we dislike. Highlight everyone's strengths, and those areas look better all the time.

Map out stepparents

A relief map has protruding areas to show where the mountains and valleys are located. With a quick look, the reader can see which areas are difficult and which might be easily passable.

Make a mental relief map of each stepparent and learn to respect it. What are his highs and lows? What makes him happy and what makes him blue? Smart people head for the happy and stay away from the blue.

The differences between the two homes are obvious. At one place you eat hamburgers in the living room; at the other it's steaks on the good dishes. At one house it's creamed broccoli; at the other it's baked beans. In one home the discipline is tough; at the other there is hardly any at all.

Figure out ways to get along with each stepparent. It takes double the effort, but the rewards are twice the gain.

When a young person is too rigid, he creates a terrible atmosphere. Everyone needs to bend or even twist to the different personalities involved. Flexibility will be the key in dealing with so many changing people.

Learning to Speak Up!

What do you do when something is bugging you? How do you inform parents that you are going crazy because of the rules, curfews, guidelines, or whatever?

Many teenagers do one of two things. They stuff all their complaints and grind them up inside, or they save them up and scream and shout later. They are called Pouters or Shouters.

Neither type is the best. The best communicators are open and honest talkers. They explain how they feel in direct conversation. Good communicators don't run people off or scare them away. Neither do they clam up and hope people will know how to interpret their silence.

Let's look at some ways to speak so people will listen.

Eleven terrible ways to communicate

- Screaming and walking out of the room
- Accusing or attacking people
- Throwing the cat across the room

- Digging up last month's problems
- Name calling
- The silent treatment
- Sweeping generalities ("She always gets her way. I never get my way. You are all dumb.")
- Filling the sugar bowl with salt
- Threatening to run away
- Saying, "You aren't really my parent, anyway."
- Hiding garlic under the car seat

Twelve great ways to communicate

- Ask for time out to talk.
- Be calm.
- Talk to the person or people who are part of the problem.
- Define the problem specifically; be precise.
- Confine your remarks to the particular problem.
- Discuss the problem without smearing the person.
- Take time to listen to their response.
- Be prepared to compromise.
- Handle one problem at a time when you can. Ten at a time becomes overwhelming.
- Ask to speak to the entire family together if it affects everyone.
- Work toward a solution.
- Agree to meet again to talk further.

When to complain

Real problems

Don't be a chronic complainer. After a while, everyone will tune you out.

If it is a problem to you

It is a real problem. Don't be too bashful to explain what hurts you.

Don't swallow every injustice

If it's important, speak up very clearly.

Keep the list short

If the problem needs fixing, say so; if not drop it from the list. Don't keep adding to a list longer than a bedsheet.

You could be helping everyone

People who speak up don't need to feel foolish about it. When we keep our feelings hidden, we hurt all our relationships. Do your family a favor and explain clearly your emotional rash. It needs to be taken care of so your family can have the most tranquility possible.

Looking for Love

We all want to be loved. When we hit the teen years, the quest for love becomes strong. Love is powerful and all of us need it. We want other people to love us because love makes us feel valuable. And it isn't just boy/girl love.

If a parent loves us, we feel important. When a parent seems to reject us we feel hurt. Parental love is high on the list of needs for most of us.

When parents move out and move in, divorce and remarry, call or don't call, it's hard to know if any real love exists. Changing relationships tend to leave love up in the air. When the family is torn apart we need lots of reassurance that love is still there.

A stepparent isn't a date

Love takes time. We learn to love people as we get to know them. A stepparent isn't a date who loves you at first sight. They may like you and enjoy being around you, but love is a feeling that grows. True love needs two ingredients: time and experience. The more a stepparent gets to know you, the more likely he is to love you.

Love is highly manageable. If a stepparent chooses to love you and you let him love you, love will probably happen. Read that sentence again.

Anna was a stepdaughter who decided to show her mean side. Whenever her stepfather tried to get to know her, she turned tough, harsh, and prickly. In Anna's mind she decided that if he really loved her, he should be able to tolerate her dark moods.

She built barriers and dared her stepfather to climb over them. Anna wanted to be loved, but she wanted to make loving her a hard thing to do.

Her stepfather repeatedly tried to climb the walls, wade the rivers, and dodge the darts. He wanted to love a girl who was trying her best to make it difficult.

This maneuver is very common among teenagers, especially if they don't like themselves. They ask someone to go an extra mile to prove their love.

It isn't fair. It's downright cruel. When someone is trying to get close to us, we shouldn't roll rocks down the hill to discourage him or knock him down.

Love is like a building

If we constructed a block building, we would have to add one block at a time. Love is often like that. We don't say "Presto!" and make the entire structure leap onto the lot. The building blocks are tolerance, patience, listening, sharing, laughing, and many more. One by one we pile them on top of each other. Before long we start to see a shape come together. Soon we recognize the shape as love.

Allow your stepparent time to build love one block at a time. Each day or month he or she may love you more and you will enjoy watching it develop.

Sometimes love develops and we refuse to use it. The new parent could be doing, saying, and feeling all the right things, but his or her love is being rejected. When love is sent, it must be received. Love could be all around us, but we turn our backs as if it doesn't exist.

Give everyone time, because love usually takes time. Be willing to receive genuine love when it is offered.

What if love doesn't come?

That could happen. We would be dishonest if we didn't admit that this is possible. Many stepparents and stepteens never fully connect. Every teenager who pays attention knows this.

But many stepparents and stepteens do come to appreciate, enjoy, and even love each other.

There is something more important than love. The foundation to every meaningful relationship is respect. If we have no respect for the other, we can't expect to become close. We can tolerate, be polite, or "stomach" each other, but a genuine relationship is impossible without respect. We are all due a certain amount of dignity simply because we are human beings.

Our first and primary goal is respect. Stepparents need to place value on what their stepteen feels, hopes, and does. If a stepparent continuously bashes what a teenager counts as valuable, the relationship will not connect. The same is true if a teenager belittles what his stepparent feels, hopes, and does. A lack of respect, wrecks the relationship.

Begin at the foundation level. Don't try to put the roof on first. Show respect and ask for respect. You won't ridicule them and you expect they won't ridicule you. You will look for their strengths and positive side, and they will look for yours.

Only after you are willing to show respect (the foundation) do you need to worry about love (the roof).

Someone tells me, "I don't like anything about you. Your hair is stringy, your breath is bad, your socks sag, your friends stink, your jokes are awful, your television shows are terrible, and your hobby is ridiculous; but remember, I love you."

That kind of love is hard to accept and believe. If you don't like anything about me, if you think I'm worthless, where is the love?

Begin with worth

Make a short list. What is it that you respect your step-parent for? She is

- caring
- friendly
- thoughtful
- polite
- generous
- humorous
- accepting
- cheerful
- active
- adventuresome

Start with just three or four. As time goes on, add to the list and watch it grow. A foundation is being built. At the same time the stepparent is learning to respect you. This sounds like the beginning of a relationship that could turn into love.

But what if it doesn't? Suppose you never really love each other. Maybe there is too much pain, too many disruptions, too much confusion; for whatever reason it simply doesn't happen. In that case, be happy for respect. Be glad that you can value each other anyway.

Before Vickie actually met her stepfather she used to see him sort of "creeping" around the house. Actually, he would sit in the car and wait for her mother to come out. Her parents had agreed to separate but were still living at home.

Each time Vickie saw this man waiting in the car, she realized how much she hated him.

Nine months later, that same man became her stepfather. She certainly didn't love him. Vickie saw him as a big part of the problem.

Despite that shaky start, fifteen-year-old Vickie tried to respect him. She looked for his good points and found them. They never got to the place of loving each other, but they did begin to find value.

Aim for mutual respect. If that builds into love, you have a bonus. If it doesn't, at least you have grown to appreciate one another.

Happy About the Split?

When my parents divorced, I was fourteen. Unlike many teenagers, I thought it was a great idea. I can't remember one happy day in the life of my parents. They may have enjoyed each other before I was born, but I never saw it.

Naturally I wish it had been different. I, too, dreamed of a neat little family laughing, going places together, and standing arm in arm for great family pictures. That dream never came true.

The loss still hurts, but not because of the divorce. Our family never happened. That's what feels so bad. The divorce was more like finally burying a body that had died a long time ago.

Many teenagers are devastated by their parents' divorce and remarriage. But frankly, some of us are not. We may be disappointed and crushed because the family didn't work, but the actual divorce was a relief.

Those of us who feel that way don't like to say it. We are afraid we sound like ghouls or monsters who are glad our families disintegrated. That's not the case. We would have given anything to see our families happy. But my family wasn't. And after years of pain and strain and even abuse, there was no hope.

Do we feel guilty because we are glad the family split? Sometimes. But we shouldn't feel guilty. Relief is what we honestly feel and we should be able to say so. Never feel guilty about being honest.

We don't have to run around bragging about it. There is no reason to carry a placard saying, "I'm glad they split." But when we discuss how the divorce affects us and how the remarriage affects us, go for openness and honesty.

I didn't have any strong feelings about my dad's remarriage. After all, it was his remarriage. His new wife was a good person and she helped him tremendously. We got along fine and life went on.

Don't pretend you feel one way when you feel another. That's the important rule. Most of us feel a number of ways about the entire matter.

Guilt is a tick. It buries its head inside your skin and makes you sick. Don't feel guilty because you are glad for the split.

If Your Parent Is Dead

What difference does it make what happened to your "other" parent? A teenager's "parental past" could determine how he looks at his stepparent. If your memories are good, bad, or merely empty, those factors could play a huge role in how you accept or reject a stepparent.

Lisa and Todd had seen their father only a few times in recent years. Each encounter had been unpleasant. He drank excessively and was very demanding. When their mother remarried, they looked forward to receiving a stepfather. They imagined what a good man this new parent might be.

Young people sometimes react in unpredictable ways toward their stepparents. What they expect often depends on what they experienced with their biological parents. Some expect the same relationships as they had previously; others expect the opposite.

Dave idolized his mother. He didn't want the divorce or the remarriage. He fought his stepmother from the first day she walked in the door. The only way they could become friends would be if she turned around and marched back out the door.

Smart teenagers decide to aim for peace. Even though they didn't choose this marriage, they decide to work for tranquility. They realize that everyone gets hurt in war, so they ease off and call for a truce.

If your parent died

When you have living parents, there can be serious tension between the two families. The two sets of parents often quarrel over money, holidays, the children's health, visits, and the list goes on. Special occasions can be a headache. Who sits where at the graduation? Who has the party? What about the wedding? Later all the parents and stepparents may stumble into each other at the hospital when the grandbaby is born.

But what if one of the biological parents has died? How does everyone handle the memory of a deceased parent?

Children usually have very good memories of a parent who has died. As time goes by, they concentrate on that parent's excellent qualities. They can recall her saying nice things, smiling, giving them gifts, and understanding them.

No parent is perfect, but young people tend to forget their parents' mistakes. The good times with a deceased mother become ingrained in one's mind while the bad times fade away. Consequently, teenagers often have a fantastic opinion of their dead parents. Fine! That's the way it ought to be.

But that perfect image makes it tough on a stepparent. As one stepparent said: "I have to compete every day with a dead saint." It's hard to think of a more difficult job.

To be fair, don't compare your deceased parent with your stepparent. In most cases the stepparent can't measure up. A dead parent isn't around to make new mistakes. A parent who has died can't tell you to eat your vegetables or drink your orange juice. She won't be able to ask you where you were until 1:00 A.M. She will never say anything to embarrass you in front of your friends.

Don't put your parent down, but at the same time try not to idealize her, either. Your parent wasn't perfect. In your heart you know that. We love a parent best when we accept him as both good and bad. If we love a parent because we think she was perfect, we have created a parent who is not real. Love the full, complete person—faults and all.

Don't expect your stepparent to fully appreciate how wonderful your deceased parent was. Some teenagers are upset if their stepparent doesn't praise the departed parent. A stepparent should show due respect, certainly an amount of admiration, but he can't be expected to share the same high regard you have for that person.

Feelings aren't as easy to control as behavior, so first of all ask how you act toward your stepparent. Do you act like he or she is inferior to your real parent? Do you treat him as if he isn't as good as your deceased parent? Do you talk to her without respect or consideration? Do you act like fate or God has robbed you of your real parent and replaced him with this surrogate parent? On the other hand, are you kind and respectful and understanding toward your stepparent?

No one will ever take the place of your biological parent. Don't be afraid that a stepparent will erase the memory. You may be able to accept your stepparent for who she is without hurting the image you have of your deceased parent. Both are real. Each has or had his own function and place.

To honor a stepparent does not mean we dishonor our biological parent. They are two separate people each deserving to be his or her own person. They don't need to be in competition. Neither needs to win or lose in your life. Each can be special on his or her own terms.

Let's list some of those thoughts about deceased parents and stepparents.

1. Keep your good memories.

2. No one is perfect.

3. Don't compare.

4. Don't expect your stepparent to share completely your enthusiasm for your dead parent.

5. Show respect for your parent and your stepparent.

Be sure to share some of your feelings. Tell your stepparent why you miss your parent. He or she would like to know some of the fond memories that you cherish. Friends share things like that. Simply be careful not to use your parent as a weapon to wound your stepparent.

There are a few phrases you should avoid. We all forget and say unkind things. Our tongues slip and deliver some sharp answers. Try not to say things like:

"You aren't my real mother."
> (She knows that.)

"My mother loved me."
> (As if your stepparent doesn't.)

"My father gave me anything I wanted."
> (Probably not true.)

"My mother didn't believe in curfews."
> (She may have changed her mind.)

"My father gave me alcohol."
> (Maybe he shouldn't have.)

Often we know when we are trying to hurt someone. Those things we should stop saying immediately. Other words are slip-ups, and only later do we realize how painful they are. Either way, we may need to apologize.

If we control what we say and control our behavior, we can avoid using memory as a weapon. At the same time we preserve the great feeling about a parent we love tremendously.

Your Parents' Love Life

Sixteen-year-old Heather was embarrassed when her forty-two-year-old mother became pregnant. She tried not to think about her mother's sex life, but now it couldn't be ignored. Pregnancy was like wearing a sign around her neck declaring, "Look, I've been having sex." It wasn't the kind of announcement that Heather was eager for the world to receive, especially about her "aging" mother.

Teenagers have enough trouble with their parents' outdated clothing, slow music, and corny jokes. They don't also want to have to deal with stepparents who act like they have just passed through puberty. It's hard to watch forty-year-olds cooing, nibbling, and pawing each other like a couple of adolescents. Young people don't want to go out on a mall date only to see their stepparents strolling and holding hands in the same mall. It seems unnatural.

They didn't see their biological parents go through these mating rituals. All of that took place twenty years ago, during the Ice Age, before they were born. It's hard enough trying to picture them roller-skating arm in arm in the 1970s. But this couple of lovebirds, their stepparents, are going together right in front of their teenagers' eyes.

They are in love

Fortunately, stepparents usually begin their relationship with love. We say usually because a few get married simply because they need each other. Some are looking for a father or mother for their children. That's a strong drive among divorced parents. It's hard to raise children alone. Often parents remarry with both goals in mind: They have found someone they love and they believe that person will be good for their children.

To some teenagers it looks like a purely selfish act. They may not want their parents to remarry. But the parents may see it as a package deal that is good for everyone.

The "second" love probably isn't exactly like the first one. A second marriage is usually more calculated, thought through a bit more carefully. Two of the main reasons why people remarry are companionship and help. Love is important, but now they tend to see love as commitment. Sex is significant, but not normally as high on the list as it was in the first marriage.

Second marriages tend to be wiser and more practical. Loneliness and acceptance are key factors. Those seem to be important areas for most of us. Finances may play a larger role the second time around. Parenting skills are a consideration.

It would appear that the second marriage is more a matter of the head and less of the heart. But in spite of all the thought and careful selection that goes on, second marriages have no better chance of lasting than first marriages.

For all the differences between first and second marriages, love plays a very strong part. It may be a cautious, thinking love; but it can be a deep, real love just the same.

Better for everyone

Tell yourself it's all right to have two forty-year-old love-crazy adolescents running around the house patting each other and saying, "Oh, honey bun." That may not be exactly what you want, but the longer this couple stays in love, the better it is for everybody. Encourage them. Baby-sit, if necessary. Do the dishes so they can date. Any logs you can throw on the flames of love might help keep those fires burning.

Some teenagers are threatened by the love of their step-parents. They see it as a displacement of themselves in favor of someone else.

Jessica had a close bond with her father. Her parents divorced when she was ten and her father had custody. She and her father had managed well for five years before he remarried. The introduction of a stepmother into her relationship was an unwelcome addition for Jessica. Immediately she turned hostile to her father's wife and was determined to remain that way.

She was hurt badly by the move and couldn't find any acceptable way to deal with her pain. Her bewildered father couldn't imagine why Jessica wasn't more open to a person as good as his wife.

Stepdaughters and stepmothers frequently go to war over the same father and husband. Some statistics suggest this is the most common battleground. The daughter had something special and this new person seems to disrupt their relationship. Anger, resentment, and revenge are all possible because of this change.

It's hard to see at the time, but a sincere love interest could be the best thing that could happen to her father and Jessica. The stepmother has the potential of making the father's life fuller and happier. In turn, a satisfied life can give Jessica a more well-rounded father.

Jessica may lose a few things. She should mention her need for time and attention so her father won't forget. A stepmother could add the precise ingredients that this family needs to make it balanced and caring. Jessica will have trouble seeing this at first; but if she tries to be accepting, time may demonstrate how good this new tripod can be.

Are they having sex?

Certainly! How often and when is their business, so we don't have to delve into the details. Teenagers tend to think of sex as a privilege of youth and newlyweds. Actually many middle-aged and older people have a very active sex life.

Sex in a second marriage can be more satisfying than in the first. Sometimes a person experiences a miserable time in bed during a first marriage but learns to become more caring and loving in the second.

Try not to judge your parents or their activities. These matters belong to them. What could be more frustrating than a teenager trying to police the activities of their love-struck parents and stepparents?

Your original parents no longer love each other—certainly not in the way they used to. They will not get back together, and now they have found someone new. That's their decision and not the children's. Go with the flow and be glad that your parents are in love—even if it isn't with one another.

Sexual Tensions

When Tricia was fourteen, she suddenly noticed that her thirty-five-year-old stepfather looked pretty good. A handsome man, his hair hadn't started to gray and he had a trim, strong physique. Tricia felt something for him that scared her. She wanted to be held by him. Not in the childlike way they used when they were wrestling and clowning around. Tricia began to wonder what it would be like for her stepfather to hold her close in the way a man holds a woman.

Tricia's feelings frightened her, but actually they aren't that unusual. The same crush or drive that teenagers often have for schoolteachers, principals, and youth workers can also surface around a stepparent.

All the elements are there. Teenagers are beginning to experience a growing and mysterious sex drive. Sex drives are both warm and powerful. They are at once tender and raging.

As a young person tries to sort out those feelings, an adult male or female comes into his life. The adult is new, an authority figure, and not actually related. They will live under the same roof, be around each other a great deal, share emotions, and be in physical contact.

Those factors do not create a sexual charge in everyone, but it happens in many stepfamilies. While more common between stepdaughters and stepfathers, the attraction also occurs between some stepsons and stepmothers.

The burden of sexual attraction also works in reverse. Some stepparents are sexually drawn toward their stepchildren or stepteens. Statistics are unreliable but they suggest that family sexual involvement is much more likely to occur in a stepfamily than in a traditional one. The main reason is that people live in the same house, but they are not blood relatives. The temptations are greater under those circumstances.

Not drooling monsters

None of this suggests that members of stepfamilies are sex fiends. Don't imagine that there is an extraordinary amount of panting and heavy breathing going on. But there may be heightened sexual feelings in some stepfamilies. Unfortunately, those underlying tensions can create serious problems.

In many cases the friction between a stepteen and a stepparent may be caused by their sexual attraction. Tricia may unconsciously pick battles with her stepfather as a way of fighting off her uneasy feelings toward him.

However, in some families there are monsters. A stepparent may step over the bounds of normal contact and make sexual advances toward a stepchild. If that happens, in the early stages you as a stepteen should tell him *No* in direct terms. Let him know you have no interest in any form of sexual activity with him. If the action persists or is more serious, report it to your biological parent immediately. Don't tolerate it. By reporting the event, you will at least create a family discussion and make it less likely to happen again.

If the advances continue and your biological parent refuses to take action, you may need to report it to someone else. Tell a teacher, a counselor, or a minister. In most instances, a parent should be told first; but whatever it takes, make sure you get protection. No teenager should put up with sexual advances from an adult even if it is a stepparent.

This almost certainly will not happen to you. But everyone should be informed in case it does. People with information are better able to cope with tough times should they come.

Out of balance

The potential sexual attraction between stepdaughter and stepfather creates a serious imbalance in the family. Because of real or imagined attraction between the two, several problems can arise.

- The mother may be jealous of the attention her daughter and husband show each other, even if it is innocent.
- The stepfather may try to avoid his stepdaughter because he doesn't trust his thoughts or actions.
- Stepdaughter and stepfather may treat each other briskly or harshly in an effort to build a wall of protection.
- They may be afraid to be alone in the house together.
- Innocent touching or contact may cause heightened tension when nothing was intended.
- A stepson may be frightened by his sexual thoughts about either his stepsister or his stepmother. He might feel guilty and have trouble communicating with either of them.

Awareness goes a long way. If someone is drawn to a stepfamily member and he is having friction with the same person, it may be cause and effect. A few sessions with a family counselor could bring immediate results.

Stepsiblings

Imagine this: You are a healthy, growing, sexually developing sixteen-year-old boy. Your parent remarries and soon a great-looking fifteen-year-old female moves into your home. Soon you're sharing a bathroom, sitting around watching television late in the evening, and sometimes arm wrestling at the table. She isn't really a relative and she looks like a million bucks. Will some stepbrothers begin to fantasize about their stepsisters? Will some stepsisters begin to fantasize about their stepbrothers?

In traditional or biological families the idea of kissing your sister makes most of us gag. But stepsiblings fall into another category. We may not have built up a natural barrier that kicks in and says "off limits." We may have to remind ourselves why this doesn't work.

An involvement with a stepsibling may sound simple enough. Why not date each other? What can a few dates hurt? Remember that most teen dating is terminal. It ends sometime. What will happen when you no longer want to be involved? Will you still live in the same house? Will you have emotional baggage and deep feelings? What if one of you wants to break it off and the other doesn't? How will you live under the same roof if one feels like the wounded martyr who got dumped? A romantic involvement between two teenagers who are semirelated and living in the same house is simply packed with pain.

Clothes and behavior

Despite all protests to the contrary, what we wear and when we wear it is important. With nonrelatives of the opposite sex under the same roof, everyone should think twice about what he or she wears. No one has to be prudish and wear a trench coat on the patio, but a reasonable amount of cover makes good sense.

True, if someone gets out of bounds, it is not because of the clothing you are wearing. But everyone can avoid trouble by dressing in a responsible manner. Be smart.

The same goes for how we tease and play games. It does matter how we touch each other and what we kid about. What one person sees as innocent the other may interpret as flirtatious. There is no sense in becoming fearful, but everyone should try to think about his or her actions and how they might be misunderstood.

Every bathroom must have a lock. When a stepsibling is using the bathroom, the door should be locked. The same goes for bedrooms. People of the opposite sex should not be barging into rooms without being invited. Too much looseness can turn ugly very quickly.

Discuss these rules and regulations as a family. Never take it for granted that everyone understands. When the guidelines are violated, insist on more family discussions to restate the rules.

Stepsiblings should not be allowed to continuously break the household laws. Barging in once may be a sign of thoughtlessness; but if it continues, report it immediately.

Caution without fear

The purpose of discussing sex in stepfamilies is not to set off alarms and frighten anyone. The goal is to provide information. Knowledge goes a long way toward erasing fear. Every member of the family should exercise care. We need to recognize certain boundaries and respect them.

When we know what is going on, we are better able to relax and enjoy others. Sex is a natural part of stepparenting and like a river flows best when contained within its banks.

Communication, reasonable caution, and an understanding of the ground rules will make the home's atmosphere safe and secure. If at any time you don't understand what is going on, or if you have questions about how you feel, don't be embarrassed to talk to someone about it. Hearing yourself describe the situation will help you comprehend what is going on.

Great stepfamilies have a healthy concept of where sex belongs and where it doesn't.

Too Old to Be Disciplined

If we had to name the three biggest problems in stepfamilies, one of them would be the question of discipline. Who has the right to tell whom what to do? Too many families go to war over this and never get over the battle scars. They never get close or become friends or even respect each other because they stay angry over the discipline thing.

The good news is that some families have found ways to handle discipline smoothly. Not that they don't have conflict, but they have devised methods to deal with their disagreements in a constructive fashion.

Discipline doesn't have to result in contempt for each other. Unfortunately, it often does. But it doesn't have to.

Discipline problems are normal

Almost all families have discipline problems—traditional families, single-parent families, adoptive families, foster families, broken families, stepfamilies, and any other kind we might think of. Discipline is a messy business. It amounts to one person trying to control another. Not many of us like being controlled by someone else.

Even if we had an ideal family (whatever in the world that is), discipline would aggravate us. We don't want anyone telling us to pick up our socks or to be home by midnight.

The temptation is to feel sorry for ourselves because we are steps. But remember, we don't like our bio-parents bossing us around either.

Before we say, "It's terrible having a stepparent telling me what to do," let's be fair and admit that we don't like any parent disciplining us. Even when we know that control is good for us, we don't want someone doing it.

The stepparent problem is too often exaggerated. We need to keep it in perspective. Stepparent discipline is enough of an ordeal without blowing it out of proportion.

Core of the problem

When Mother marries George, he becomes an adult figure around the house. George tries to be easygoing and friendly to the stepteen. Suddenly one day George gets a stern look on his face and says, "Listen here, young lady, you be in this house by midnight or else. And I don't want to hear another word about it."

What happened? Whatever became of affable old George? The father/protector/authority figure in George comes to the top. He becomes tired of giving and taking and trying to be kind. Enough of this baloney, he decides; you do it because I said to, he demands.

The minute he says it, the stepteen says in the back of her mind, "You aren't my father; how dare you tell me what to do!" And sometimes a teenager says this aloud and stuns everyone.

George feels the need to exercise authority. His stepteen believes it is unfair and cruel to have her stepparent tell her what to do.

These two opposite opinions will repeatedly run into conflict unless the core of the problem is resolved. Smart families work out the details and try to define the boundaries of discipline. Painful families yell at each other and try to verbally beat the other into submission.

The best discipline

Whenever Dan went to a party, he always came home thirty minutes late. He could have come home on time, but the thought of obeying a parent was more than he could cope with. His goal was more than independence. He wanted something different than just a good time. Dan was into defiance for defiance' sake. He wanted to "prove" something: that no one could tell him what to do.

Dan didn't have a stepparent problem. He had an authority problem.

We resolve a large number of our difficulties if we discipline ourselves. Keep decent hours, get acceptable grades, show up for meals, shovel a path in the bedroom, share a few plans with the family, and don't keep livestock in the basement. When we refuse to take care of ourselves, we are asking someone else to take care of us.

Where a stepparent messes up

Too many stepparents believe they may simply speak and their stepteen will accept those words as marching orders. If the young person refuses to obey, the adult believes it is an insult to his authority and he gets bent out of shape.

The adult pictures herself walking into a stepfamily and instantly becoming a traditional or biological parent. No one told her that this doesn't usually work. When the teenager resists this authority figure, the stepparent tries desperately to force the issue and demand obedience. The very tone of demanding obedience turns the stepteen off.

Cody from Illinois said that when he became a stepfather, he tried being bossy. When his teenage stepdaughter left her room messy, he flew into a rage. Today Cody has mellowed out and become a terrific parent. When he sees his stepdaughter's messy room, he simply closes the door.

That piece of wisdom didn't come easily to him. The family had to discuss the matter and reach decisions on how he might handle situations that he doesn't like.

Try to be patient with a new parent. He needs to learn a different style of family than he expected.

Family discussions

Be patient while everyone learns. Get together as a family and discuss how the discipline will work. How would you like to see it come together?

Here are some suggestions and guidelines for your family discussion. Talk about these statements.

1.   Don't model your discipline after a traditional family; you aren't one.

2.   Most major discipline should come through the bioparent.

3.   Work on friendship between stepparent and stepteen. You will accomplish more if you like each other.

4. Encourage parents to get their act together. It isn't helpful if they argue over discipline in front of the teenagers.

5. Become educated. Read a book. Find a support group. Talk to other stepfamilies. Don't learn everything by trial and error.

6. Make the rules and regulations together. The teenager should help decide the consequences if he or she comes in late.

7. Call a family meeting. If something is in danger of getting out of hand, tell everyone you have to talk.

8. Start a group of steps at school, at church, or at a neighborhood community center. Ask an adult to sponsor. Talk about how they deal with discipline.

9. Be constructive. Tell them what will work. What is the best way to correct a situation or behavior? Don't just say, "Leave me alone."

Keep your sense of humor

Everyone makes mistakes. Stepparents will say the wrong things at the wrong times. They will butt in when they should have stayed out. Don't make a federal case out of every slip. While stepparents aren't a laughing matter, they do some highly laughable things.

If they bark about leaving cups and glasses in the television room, pick them up. There's no need to argue. Neither should you get an attitude. Don't sweat the small stuff. If they ask you to put the newspaper on the coffee table, don't toss it on the chair out of defiance. Touchiness will only keep everyone in turmoil.

Look for the humor and stay in a good mood. Everyone needs to lighten up and stay happy.

Do You Ever Think of Running Away?

A movie star recently said he owed a great deal to his stepmother. Because she was so mean, he ran away from home at age fourteen and eventually ended up in acting.

There is a great deal of bitterness in what the actor said. He went through some rough experiences trying to hold his life together: working at odd jobs and living under tough conditions.

Many young people think about bailing out of their stepfamilies. They believe they can't take the pressure any more, and hitting the road sounds like a better choice. Most young people think about running away sometime. In stepfamilies the temptation may be a little greater. During their high school years, the thought probably occurs to them more than once. When they finish school, stepteens are quick to leave home.

The problem is that for every young person who became a movie star there are thousands who didn't. Many of them ended up:

- homeless
- raped
- jailed

- on drugs
- hungry
- robbed

- prostitutes
- sick
- dead

As a policeman said, after two weeks on the streets a teenager will never be the same. When he runs out of food and money, he will do almost anything to survive.

Just seeing a runaway on film doesn't do it. You can't feel his emptiness, fear, hunger, desperation, nausea, and feeling of hopelessness. Any show that glorifies the life of a runaway has done a great disservice to teenagers.

Other alternatives

What do we do when we are stretched like an overinflated balloon? We feel like we will blow up if something doesn't change. The question is, How do we change the situation without doing anything we might regret?

Four rules for running away

Rule Number One

Don't run away.

Rule Number Two

Look for a way to make adjustments. Talk Talk Talk.

Tell people what is bugging you and discuss ways to make changes. Some things that look impossible usually have solutions if you work together to find the answers.

When we stop talking, we begin to imagine that there are no options. If we feel there are no options, we start to think about hitting the highway.

Leaving home is such a traumatic, life-altering decision that it cannot be done lightly. Any young person who goes into a rage and stomps out, determined to never return, enters a risk zone.

Some teenagers protest that they have tried over and over to communicate, but it never works. Relationships often take a great deal of negotiating and repeated attempts at problem-solving. Expect to feel frustrated, but still keep working at it.

If necessary, suggest that a third party be contacted to help resolve your differences. Counselors, ministers, social workers, relatives, youth workers, even mutual friends might be good mediators who can listen to both sides and help guide you to solutions.

Creative problem-solving can be fun even in some of the most stressful situations. Take pride in your ability to reach a middle ground during tough negotiations. There are some things parents won't budge on and shouldn't budge on. Parents need to say no sometimes, but many other things are adjustable if everyone is willing to keep talking.

Rule Number Three

If you decide to leave, have some definite safe place to go. Never hit the streets on your own.

Some teenagers who read this book are going to leave home. That's too bad, but it's true. Maybe they are being molested and abused. Maybe they feel that they have run out of options and can't stay any longer.

If you are going to leave, be sure you have a place to go. Talk to a family member, a counselor, a minister, or someone who can make arrangements for housing. Have a mature adult contact who can help you reason this out. That person could save you from making some terrible decisions.

Find a safety net before you go out on the high wire. Life is lonely enough without taking this risk at age fifteen.

Rule Number Four

Don't feel too bad because you think about running away.

This doesn't mean you have the worst family in the world. It doesn't mean you are sick or necessarily that your family members are sick.

It's possible to think about running away and still love the people you want to leave. You may love them but feel you can't live with them. You might believe they have the worst set of rules in the civilized world and you can't stand it any longer.

We can say to ourselves that we have thought about running away but we still have a decent family and we are still decent people. Most of us have thought our families are outdated, old-fashioned, mixed up, and half-crazy. But in calmer moments we have also seen how loving and accepting they can be.

The temptation passes away

For most, the thought of running away is a passing impulse. But well over a million young people do take the leap. A great many return home the same night and many are back in their own beds within a day or two. Unfortunately, hundreds of thousands of teenagers remain on the streets. They are the ones who go through the horrible experiences.

If you are planning on running, you do have a real problem. No one should laugh at your predicament. For a while at least, you feel like there is no other way out. But there are usually options, and most teenagers find other avenues to solve their family difficulties.

Problem Solving

How long did you live with one parent? For months or years? Your family had one adult in residence plus one or more children of different ages.

Who made most of the decisions while there was one parent at home? Did the one adult make most of the major decisions, or was decision making a shared process? Were you treated like a young adult? Did your parent ever depend on you to make some of the decisions?

In some homes twelve-year-olds are put in charge. Tired of solving problems by themselves, some parents ask their children to help pick out an apartment, select a car, plan menus for the week. Boys are often told they will have to be the "man of the house." Girls are told to watch the younger children, clean the house, and start the meals.

When your parent married or remarried, the family structure changed. The problem-solving, decision-making power base took on a different approach. How will you get things done in this new, two-adult family?

Understanding those changes and adapting to them are very important to your happiness and well-being.

Feeling displaced

When Matt's mother remarried, he felt shut out. Yesterday he was the "man of the house." Now his stepfather seems to replace Matt in the family, and the thirteen-year-old boy got dumped back into being just a kid again.

Being displaced or dropped on the totem pole hurt Matt. It was as if he had been replaced in the family and in his mother's life. He didn't like his new role, and his unhappiness was obvious to everyone.

On the other hand, Robin loved being displaced. She saw herself as the maid, babysitter, part time cook, counselor, and head interior decorator. Her new stepmother was no threat at all. Robin was glad to turn over all the decision-making and problem-solving to this lady.

Some are sad and some are glad. Some resent the shift while others welcome it.

Stepfamilies are like small rowboats. When one or two new people get on board, those already on board may have to shift their weight. The vessel will not be safe unless some people make adjustments.

Expect a new way of problem-solving. The new way may not be better than the old but it almost certainly will be different.

Don't be afraid

Change may not be easy, but change can be beneficial. Don't assume that you will never get your way again. Under the new system of problem-solving you may end up with more of your problems solved. Your best interests and your goals may be more likely to happen with a two-adult family.

Teenagers who throw up their hands and reject the step-family lessen their chances of getting things done. Those who accept the new situation and work with it end up better fulfilled. Each young person has to make the important choice: cooperate or don't cooperate.

Be optimistic! Give your input as to how decisions will now be made around this house. If you wimp out and refuse to say anything, you relinquish your opportunity to help solve problems. A tight-lipped teenager sitting on the couch and refusing to say anything is unlikely to have his real problems addressed.

Watch the problem-solving shift

When your parent remarries, the decision-making process takes a different turn. Yesterday your parent looked more to the children for advice or approval. Today your parent will lean more on the new spouse. That's good. Your parent needed a companion to bounce decisions off. A forty-year-old parent and a fourteen-year-old don't always make the best partners.

Adults who love each other will share most of the process. Be happy for this. Your parent needed someone her own age to talk to. Hopefully they will remain good for each other and carry each other's burdens. Ideally they will share their problem-solving.

Don't back off

This step becomes vital. It would be easy to withdraw from the family and act like an outsider. Don't do that. Let the adults know that you want to be part of your own decision-making process. Tell them you are not content to let two forty-year-olds make decisions for you. Ask to be a partner in the family council.

You want family meetings. You promise to attend them. You agree to speak up, furnish ideas, and make your real wants known. You have a stake in the present and future choices that are made by this family. Tell them you want to be part of it.

Families of all kinds get along better when everyone feels they have plenty of say in the decision process. No one wants Dad to come home and announce, "Pack up, we're moving to Anchorage."

Shared power

Most families are aware that they must consider everyone's feelings, hopes, and dreams. This is especially true of stepfamilies. There is no well-recognized chief. Not that there is no one in charge and the home is bedlam. But one of the clear strengths of a healthy stepfamily is the ability to share the power and decision-making.

We become the counselors and advisors of one another. No tyrants or dictators need to show up. We expect parents to loosen the controls and share the power. Teenagers need to do the same. If young people exercised control in the single-parent relationship, they must move toward cooperative decision-making.

Female power

In single-parent families teenage girls are frequently given control over domestic areas. They tend to clean, care for siblings, and cook. Their decision-making affects daily routines. If a male stepparent enters the family, the change may not be drastic. However, if a female stepparent joins the family, the stepdaughter may be quickly out of work.

The loss of domestic control may be traumatic. On the other hand, she might be ecstatic to finally throw off the responsibility.

Male power

Teenage boys are more apt to be in control of big-ticket items. They might do the upkeep on the car, adjust the VCR, and fix simple plumbing problems. Their parents are likely to consult them about the "big picture": Where do they move? Is it time to buy a new refrigerator? Do they need more locks on the doors? Do they have enough insurance?

When a new parent arrives, the teenager might resent losing his place of influence. This could result in a power struggle between the two males in the household. They may have to share power more than they want.

No matter what issues are involved, the biggest will probably be personal control. Will you be allowed to jointly make decisions that affect your own life?

The Stepfamily Pie

How would you describe your relationship to your stepfamily? Have you ever sat down and tried to figure out where you fit in the picture and how you relate to every one? Whom do you need to draw closer to in order for everyone to get along?

The following pie describes how most teenagers fit into the family. There are other possibilities; maybe you don't squeeze exactly into this picture. However, it gives us a starting place and you can allow for your different situation.

Find yourself in the picture.

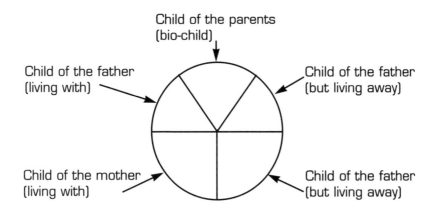

The Stepfamily Pie

If you live in two stepfamilies, make a pie for each family. After you draw your pie, add any notes you think are needed, such as: adopted, second or third divorce, parent deceased. We come in many varieties and packages. Because of special circumstances, you might not be living with either biological parent.

Bio-child

Many young people are not stepteens, but they live in a stepfamily. Their parents have been married before to someone else. Even though they are the children of this union, their life is complicated by the stepfamily factor.

Often they feel the most secure. They tend to attach more closely to both parents. However, they are very aware that families do break up and may wonder about their parents' future.

If they have grown up with stepsibs, they may have adjusted well to the situation. The best way to find out is for a bio-teen to talk about his feelings. No one can be sure how he thinks until he starts saying it out loud.

As with most teenagers there is friction with their parents. That same friction might exist with or without their stepfamilies.

Mother-child

Major nurturing in the family usually comes from Mother. They seem to care more if we are bleeding, whether we have eaten lunch, or if we have clean underwear. Often mothers tend to be better listeners and communicators.

Occasionally we find fathers who are excellent nurturers, but that's not usual. They are more often into events and things.

Life goes more smoothly for young people who do not alienate themselves from their mothers and stepmothers. If you are at war with your female parents, you miss out on many nurturing strengths that will help in the teen years and later.

Just as parents should try to stay in loving communication with their children and stepchildren, so should smart teenagers make the extra effort to get along with mothers and stepmothers. They don't hold grudges and they forgive easily. They look for ways to keep the communication open and they express their appreciation. Though they have differences, they refuse to allow a wide gap to separate them.

In a world with plenty of trouble, we are foolish to burn bridges that connect us to loving people. Burned bridges are difficult to repair.

To war with mothers and stepmothers is to mess up your own nest. If at all possible do positive things that will keep the two of you close.

Father-child

Dads come in all colors and sizes. No two are exactly alike. Some will spend hours talking to you, taking you places, listening, and being available. But most will not.

Fathers and stepfathers tend to center their lives on their jobs. Jobs are extremely important to men. The problem is that many fathers would rather work than have interchanges with their families. On the average they talk to their teenagers a bare few minutes a day. When they do talk, it is often about machines, things, events, and baseball statistics. This serves as a cover so they won't have to get personal.

Too often a man hides behind gifts. He would rather buy his child a football, a set of barbells, a stereo, or a car rather than deal with personal problems. If the teenager has a conflict, Dad may want to solve it by giving an object.

Fathers also have a nasty habit of disappearing. They go away on sales trips, on fishing trips, and to seminars. Sometimes teenagers don't hear from them for days or weeks.

Smart teenagers keep contact with their fathers and stepfathers as much as possible. Fathers are not only necessary as providers, but they help as role models, companions, and adult friends. They may also give good advice if a young person asks for it.

Wherever you fit in the stepfamily pie, let your father or stepfather know he is important. If he feels unnecessary and unwanted, he tends to fade into the background. Help him keep an active presence by reminding him that you need a close father-type.

The relationship between a father and child should not rest solely on the shoulders of the teenager. Some father-types are impossible. But smart teenagers make sure they do their part to let dads or stepdads know how much they want them around.

Why stepfamily pie?

Don't look at the graph and simply put yourself into a category. The purpose of the pie is to furnish an overview of where you stand. From that position, who is it that you need to draw closer to? No parent or stepparent is unimportant. Each of them adds or detracts from your life, and you theirs.

Make your move toward the people who are part of your developing years. Don't wait for them to move close to you.

Invite Your Stepparents Along

Deena was excited about her band concert. She was second-chair flute and loved playing her instrument. The band had practiced for months and she thought they sounded pretty good.

As soon as she learned the concert date, Deena invited her parents. She knew they wouldn't sit together, but she wanted both of them there. Deena had long ago stopped trying to bring the two back together but she was tickled when they could come to the same event.

On the afternoon of the concert Deena hurried straight home from school. As she dashed past the living room she saw Brenda, her stepmother.

"Oh," Deena shouted, "you're coming to the band concert, aren't you?"

"Well," Brenda replied sheepishly, "only if you really want me to."

"Want you to? Of course I want you to. Don't be silly," Deena paused.

"I guess I wasn't sure if I was invited," Brenda tried not to sound hurt.

"Did I forget to invite you? Well, I just assumed you would be there," Deena said, rushing off to her room.

Ghost parents

Too often stepparents become ghost parents. They live with us and help us and yet we tend to see through them. It's as though we take them for granted while we treat others as special.

Brenda ironed Deena's dress for the concert. Brenda had helped pay for the flute. On cold, wintry mornings Brenda drove Deena to early practices. But when the final time arrived, Deena's mother and father received special, personal invitations, and Brenda was treated like the maid.

What would have happened if Brenda had sat at home on the concert night? What if she had felt unwanted because she was uninvited? That would have led to all kinds of hurt feelings and misunderstandings.

Extra encouragement

Because Brenda is a stepmother, she isn't always sure when she is welcome. Even bio-parents aren't always certain if their teenagers want them around. With stepparents it is doubly difficult.

Some stepparents simply go to everything and don't care if they are wanted or not. But others look for some reassurance, maybe extra encouragement that they should be there.

Stepfamilies often spend years trying to define themselves. Each person is searching for exactly where they fit in relationship to the others in the group. The questions of who accepts whom and under what conditions keep popping up in their heads.

One way to ease that tension is for family members to go toward each other. Deena should leave no doubt in Brenda's mind that she definitely, absolutely wants her at that concert.

Teenagers are busy

Two things seem to occupy teenagers' minds. One, they have a great deal to do. Some young people race from dawn to dusk. Two, they worry a lot about themselves. With so many changes going on, they seem preoccupied with their own situations. That makes sense.

In Deena's case, both are true. She is accomplishing many things and she wants her two parents to come and see her perform.

With that much going on, it is easy to forget to touch some of the important bases. Stepparents are some of those bases.

Deena is probably thoughtful most of the time, but she isn't always careful. Adults have the same problem and they have to work on it, too.

Taken for granted

Write this on the back of your hand: No one, absolutely no one, wants to be taken for granted. "Thank you" and "Please" are appreciated by everyone.

Stepparents seem to just be there. Whatever their contributions to the family, they are often overlooked. Some can't do anything right because the stepkids refuse to accept them. Some stepparents have lived with years of coolness and rejection.

Teenagers can be excellent bridge builders. They are old enough to invite their stepparents to ball games, church events, concerts, movies, and loads of other things. But they need to take the special effort to make them feel special.

Stepparents frequently find themselves standing around on one foot wondering where they belong. When the stepchildren are in the hospital or at graduation or being married, what is a stepparent supposed to do? Does he stand beside his stepchild or is he always three paces off to the left while the bio-parents stand together?

We reduce the awkwardness by speaking up and clearing the air. "Be sure and be there," or "Remember I want you both there" might be the right phrases.

The post-concert hug

Different strokes for different folks, but keep this in mind: During the rush to thank people after a big event, it is easy to forget a stepparent. That's part of taking them for granted. If you took the time to invite them, now make the effort to thank them for coming.

If you hurry over to hug each bio-parent, don't forget to give a scrunch to your stepparent, too. Be an equal rib crusher. Don't worry how your steps and bios feel about each other. That's their turf and not yours. Be true to yourself and to your relationships. If you are grateful to a stepparent, show your appreciation and affection. Honest and open is where it is.

Don't make it a choice

Would you rather have your bio-parents or your stepparents at your special event? If there is a dumb question, this is it. Parents and stepparents should never be placed in competition or comparison. You may want each parent there for a different reason. Frankly, you may not want either one of them there. But don't make that a competitive question. Weigh each parent on his or her own merits and invite them all.

Isn't it awkward to have bio-parents and stepparents at the same occasion? Probably. Awkwardness is not the worst thing that can happen. If some uneasiness is the price to pay to have two people you love come to the event, then some awkwardness is worth it.

Let them decide

Don't make decisions for your parents. You could agonize for days trying to figure out what each of them wants and how they feel. Invite everyone you want to be there and let them decide what they will do.

Adults are too big to protect. You could get an ulcer making decisions for others. Lay it out in a straight line. "Mom, I'd love to have you there next Tuesday. Yes, Brenda is planning on being there, but I would enjoy having you in the audience."

You may have to be traffic director a few times. If your bio and step each want to get together with you afterwards for ice cream but they can't stand each other, you may need to suggest lunch or dinner for one of them before the event. Now you are the diplomat and you can put your good skills to work.

In a perfect world we might have had everything run smoothly, but none of us has a perfect world. Sometimes we have to patch and mend and make a quilt-family. Where I live, quilts are beautiful and very valuable. They take time to create and often many hands go into making them the prizes they are.

Quilt-families are worth all the extra effort because of all the good they can do.

Questions and Answers

Q. I don't like to visit my father's house. How do I let him know?

A. You have two routes to choose. One, make suggestions to your father about making your visits more fun. What would you like to do? Two, cut back on your amount of visits and their length.

Q. My mother always bad-mouths my father when I go to see her.

A. Ask her to stop that. Explain that her comments only make life tougher for you.

Q. I am fifteen and my stepdad wants to adopt me. I don't know what to say.

A. Adoption is a legal action. Your biological father will lose control over you and will almost certainly drop any financial support. If you want to strengthen your ties with your stepdad and further separate yourself from your bio-father, this could be the step to take.

Ask to have all the details spelled out to you.

Q. My grandparents haven't called for at least six months. Should I contact them?

A. Yes.

Q. My real dad sends child support, but I don't have any good clothes. Where does the money go?

A. Ask your mother. Does it go for food or housing or school or what? You also should know if your dad is actually sending the money.

Q. I'm afraid that my stepdad is starting to touch me too much.

A. Tell your mother immediately. This could be innocent, but don't wait to find out. Maybe the three of you need to discuss it right away.

Q. When my stepsister lives with us on the weekends I keep losing money. Should I confront her?

A. Yes! Explain the problem. But don't make any accusations. That should solve it. If not, go to your parents.

Q. I don't like the way my stepmother slurps her food at the table. What should I do?

A. Forget it. Save your battles for the really important issues.

Q. My father has asked me not to call my mother. What should I do?

A. Ask your father why. Then explain to him why calling is important to you. In almost all cases a young person should be allowed to talk to his mother.

Q. Why didn't my mother seek custody of me? Someone said it makes her look bad.

A. There are many good reasons why mothers do not seek custody. The real answer can be found by asking her.

Q. My parents are divorced, and so are my grandparents. What are the chances that I will get divorced too?

A. Each of us is an individual. Your marriage might stick together for fifty happy years. None of us is programmed for divorce.

Q. When I visit my dad, his girlfriend usually spends the weekend there, too. Should I tell him how wrong this is?

A. Let your father be responsible for his own moral decisions. It doesn't usually help if a teenager tries to tell an adult how to live.

Q. My stepsister is starting to look pretty good to me. Am I kinky, weird, or what?

A. Not at all. But remember, a dating relationship with a sib can be complicated and painful. You are sort of related, but you're not. Better let your heart wander elsewhere.

Q. I'm sixteen and want to go to college someday. Whose obligation is it to send me?

A. It may not be anyone's obligation. The real question is whether or not anyone is going to help. Ask each parent how it's going to work. If they aren't going to be in on it, ask them to help you get grants and loans. Either way, it's time to start finding out.

Q. If my mother gets pregnant now, I would be embarrassed to death. Shouldn't someone tell them not to do that?

A. Sorry! They're going to make that decision without you.

Q. We need another bathroom in this house. How do I persuade anybody about that?

A. Offer to help build one in the basement.

Q. How can I get my parents off my back about helping around the house?

A. Help around the house.

Q. What if a stepbrother is lying to his parents? Should I tell them what's happening?

A. Not usually. Unless there is some real danger involved, don't become a policeman to your sibs.

Q. I hate Christmas. What if I ask both families to cancel it this year?

A. It doesn't sound like Christmas is the real problem. You could get rid of Easter, Valentine's Day, Thanksgiving, and Ground Hog Day and still have the same problems. Work on trust and understanding and the holidays will get better, too.

Q. My parents have been divorced and remarried a long time, but I still cry myself to sleep half the time. What should I do?

A. You need someone to talk to. Pick out a friend, a counselor, a teacher, or a minister and tell them about it. It's hard to handle grief alone, and you are still grieving.

Q. I'm still angry at Denny for marrying my mom. If he hadn't come along, my parents might have gotten back together.

A. Don't try to judge the actions of adults. They made their decisions based on what they knew. Accept Denny as he is today. Don't try to play "what if." It's a game that no one wins.

Q. My dad wants me to push my mother to let me move in with him. How do I do that?

A. Slowly. Why does he want you to move? What are the legal questions? Are you being used as a weapon to hurt your mother? This question leaves me with a lot of questions.

Q. My mother says terrible things about my stepmother, who seems pretty neat to me. What should I do?

A. Tell your mother you don't want to hear about it.

Q. When I'm eighteen I plan to leave my mother and move in with my father. Don't you think my mother will understand?

A. The first question is, do you understand what you are doing? Why are you so determined to make the move? Is it because your father has money and no sense of discipline? Is it because your mother has little money and has to lay down the rules?

Take a piece of paper and list the reasons why you want to move. Be fair and level-headed. Just don't make a wrong move for the wrong reasons.

Q. How do I know this second marriage won't break up like the first one did?

A. You don't! Hope and pray that they will work on their love and learn from their experiences. Be as optimistic as you can and take it one day at a time.

In a Nutshell

If you have read this book to the end, you must have some great strengths. You want your situation to improve and you want your stepfamily to work. Pessimists and quitters don't read books about how to get along with others.

Because you want your family to be happy, it probably will be. It may hit some serious bumps in the road, but all families do. Over the long haul, though, you can expect a satisfying relationship of caring people. You must feel good about that.

As a teenager, you are one of the most powerful forces in your house. Your decision to use that influence cooperatively and peacefully will be great medicine for everyone.

Don't feel that the family's success depends solely on you. Everyone contributes, adds, and subtracts from the group. But your helpfulness carries a great deal of weight, just as your defiance would cause considerable damage.

When you can, go with the flow. It's easier to pitch in and make as many people as comfortable as possible. When you have to resist the waves, try to be considerate. Talk and give everyone a chance to understand how you feel. Every time you talk, you win. Talking means there is a chance that someone will see where you are coming from.

Roughly there are three kinds of stepteens:

- those at war
- those at peace
- those who are happy

The ones at war are miserable. They have to do battle every day. They are constantly drawing up strategies and figuring out how to either attack or defend.

Peaceful teens aren't looking for trouble. They enjoy the even keel. They are willing to accept the good and the bad.

Happy teens enjoy their stepfamilies. They have found ways to join in and participate. Quietly they are proud of their families.

If you aim for peaceful or happy, you will be able to draw good energy from your family. That means a lot during your teen years as well as the rest of your life.

Go for the best.

Bill Coleman

About the Author

Bill Coleman is the author of many books for young people. Having been a stepteen, Coleman has written a book for children on the subject of stepfamilies: *What Children Need to Know When They Get a New Parent*. This followed the highly successful *What Children Need to Know When Parents Get Divorced*.

Father of three, Bill and his wife, Pat, live in Aurora, Nebraska. Several of his books have been nominated for the EPA Gold Medallion and one has won. Coleman spends much of his time writing and researching. Frequently he teaches seminars, speaks at numerous other events, and appears on radio talk shows.

Enjoy these other popular titles from CompCare® Publishers!

Do I Have To Give Up Me To Be Loved By My Kids? by Jordan and Margaret Paul. The best-selling authors of *Do I Have To Give Up Me To Be Loved By You?* Jordan and Margaret Paul apply their revolutionary couples concepts to family living. *"If you have time for only one book on teen-parent relationships, pick up a copy of* Do I Have To Give Up Me To Be Loved By My Kids?*"*
—Bill Stokes, *Chicago Tribune*
#307-5, $13.99

Starving for Attention by Cherry Boone O'Neill. Cherry Boone O'Neill, daughter of Pat and Shirley Boone, nearly died after starving herself to a warped ideal of physical perfection. Thanks to the wisdom of a psychiatrist, the love of her husband and family, and her faith in God, O'Neill triumphed after a ten-year struggle with anorexia nervosa. Her personal account of the horrors of this disease makes an indispensable book for parents and young adults. **#274-5, $13.95**

Parents Who Care Too Much by James M. Farris, Ph.D. Foreword by Jack Felton, coauthor of *Toxic Faith*. A must-read book for parents whose addictive/dysfunctional child is hurling the family toward self-destruction. Family psychologist James M. Farris shows the way out of devastating code-pendency and into the healing power of love. **#275-3, $11.95**

Surviving the Prodigal Years by Marcia Mitchell. *Surviving the Prodigal Years* provides encour-agement, spiritual guidance and hope for surviving the stress-filled and often perplexing teen and young adult years. Marcia Mitchell assures her readers that although they may not be able to change the actions or attitudes of their children, they can find inner peace and strength from God to sustain them through the trials and tribulations of adolescence and young adulthood. **#284-2, $11.00**

The Adam and Eve Complex by Curtis A. Levang, Ph.D. Foreword by Jeff Van Vonderen, coauthor of *The Subtle Power of Spiritual Abuse*. Drawing on the story of Adam and Eve, psychologist Curtis A. Levang shows you how to identify shame-based thinking that can be harmful to self-esteem. His program of "graceful renewal" guides you to wholeness, authenticity, and spiritual fulfillment. If you are struggling with alienation, perfectionism, depression, anxiety, addictive/compulsive behaviors, or abusive behavior, *The Adam and Eve Complex* offers innovative, biblically based answers.
#273-7, $10.95

To order, call 1-800-328-3330 and remember to ask for your *FREE* catalog!